MUTUALITY

SUNY Series in Philosophy

Robert C. Neville, Editor

MUTUALITY

The Vision of Martin Buber

Donald L. Berry

State University of New York Press

Albany

Published by
State University of New York Press, Albany

© 1985 State University of New York

For information, address State University of New York
Press, State University Plaza, Albany, NY 12246

Library of Congress Cataloging in Publication Data

Berry, Donald L., 1925-
    Mutuality : the vision of Martin Buber

    (SUNY series in philosophy)
    Includes bibliographical references.
    1. Buber, Martin, 1878-1965. 2. Interpersonal
relations. 3. Jesus Christ—Jewish interpretations.
I. Title. II. Series.
B3213.B84B45 1984   181'.06   84-2629
ISBN 0-87395-929-9
ISBN 0-87395-930-2 (pbk.)

10 9 8 7 6 5 4 3 2 1

FOR
WANDA
MARTHA AND RUTH

Love is responsibility of an I for a Thou.

Marriage will never be given new life except by that out of which true marriage always arises, the revealing by two people of the Thou to one another.

Every real relation with a being or life in the world is exclusive. Its Thou is freed, steps forth, is single, and confronts you. It fills the heavens. This does not mean that nothing else exists; but all else lives in its light.

—Martin Buber, *I and Thou*

CONTENTS

Preface _____ ix

I. The Tree _____ xv

II. The Helper _____ 39

III. The Brother _____ 69

IV. The Vision _____ 89

Appendix _____ 99

Notes _____ 103

Index of Proper Names _____ 119

PREFACE

"In the history of the human spirit," wrote Martin Buber forty-five years ago, "I distinguish between epochs of habitation and epochs of homelessness. In the former, man lives in the world as in a house, as in a home. In the latter, man lives in the world as in an open field and at times does not even have four pegs with which to set up a tent."[1] In this century we live in just such an epoch of homelessness, and have pursued two radically different routes for personal and social renovation: the appeal to the collective, the system, the institution; and the appeal to the realm of private ecstasy, the domain of feeling, the cultivation of the interior life. These two types of salvation, the economic and the psychological, the collective and the private, could perhaps, in an extravagant way, be personified by saying that for Buber the whole of the twentieth century can be divided between Marx and Freud. Neither route leads to our becoming at home in the world.

The recovery of the sense and reality of habitation is possible, Buber suggests, only by way of dialogue, the way of mutuality. We experience life in this epoch of homelessness as depersonalized in many ways, a descent into lifeless anonymity. Many voices have alerted us to the perils of our situation, and have described its pain with ironic eloquence. Martin Buber, however, stands almost alone in his claim that the problem and its resolution are not simply or primarily concerned with the way in which we have to do with one another; the healing of modern consciousness, he suggests, cannot be achieved by attending simply to the malfunctioning of human relationships. His vision concerns the attitudes we take toward the totality of things and beings that meet us and that we meet in the world, not just inter-human realities. Buber devoted most of his attention to the possibilities of the genuine meeting between human beings. All that he said in this respect, however, needs to be heard in connection with his identification of the two basic modes of being in the world which characterize the exaltation and the melancholy of the human spirit, and the dialectical or alternating way in which these two attitudes are related.

Over against all modes of reductionism, Buber finds that the attitudes which one may take to the world of things and beings are twofold: the instrumental or objectifying ("I-It") and the reciprocal or relating ("I-Thou"). Without the objectifying work of the I-It standpoint, we could not live; but the fully human life is possible only, in addition, with dialogue of the I-Thou standpoint: ". . . without It a human being cannot live. But whoever lives only with that is not human."[2] Mutuality happens because human beings have an "instinct for communion."[3] This drive for relation, this "tender surface of personal life which longs for contact with other life,"[4] is, in Buber's words, *das eingeborene Du*,[5] "the inborn Thou," an *a priori* structure of human existing.

There are three spheres or regions, three sorts of things and beings with all of which the ways of objectifying and relating are possible. They are distinguishable only with respect to the capacity for mutuality. Mutuality is possible in varying degrees, as it arises in the sphere of nature, of human beings, and of aesthetic forms. The mutuality which is possible with other human beings provides the paradigm in light of which the limits and possibilities, the voice and the silence, of the other spheres is to be seen and heard.

In this book I do not rehearse the well-known picture of the mutuality or I-Thou relationships between two human beings which Buber draws in *I and Thou, Between Man and Man,* and in many of his other essays. Its basic features are widely familiar—spontaneous, momentary, gratuitous, orienting, wholeness of being, nonobjectifying, etc. The vision of mutuality which Buber first suggested in *Ich und Du*(1923) has become the familiar property of men and women in our time who have sought to recover the humanity obscured by the hegemony of isolating feelings and absorbing collectivities. Indeed, its successful application to the various areas of human life and work has more than confirmed the early judgment of J. H. Oldham: "I question whether any book has been published in the present century the message of which, if it were understood, would have such far reaching consequences for the life of our time."[6]

In the present work, however, I do look at three areas of Buber's thought of which insufficient notice has been taken. In Chapter One, "The Tree," I try to show how Buber's underlying vision of mutuality can expand our care for the things and beings of the natural world if it be attended to with sufficient seriousness. In Chapter Two, "The Helper," I investigate Buber's claim that those human relationships which are constituted or defined by a task to be performed are prevented normatively from achieving full mutuality (the physician-patient, the teacher-student, and the priest-penitent). In Chapter Three, "The Brother," I examine Buber's attempt to recover the figure of the Jewish Jesus. Buber's concern was always for persons and communities to be together with each other, not just to exist alongside one another, or to live in separation from each other. Consequently, he sought to bring Judaism and Christianity into a better relationship by considering Jesus not as a problem for Jewish life but as an ecumenical opportunity and task. In the concluding chapter, "The Vision," I set these three inquiries in relation to one another and to Buber's central insight.

In all of this I am not unmindful of Buber's wont to appeal to the imagination and to the intellect, to evoke and to illuminate, not just to persuade or to convince. He once said of himself that he understood his work to be leading people to a window, and inviting them to look out with him; perhaps standing there others could come to share his way of seeing and loving the world. I shall be content if in any small way I can direct the reader to that window.

In this study I draw upon both of the presently available English translations of *Ich und Du:* the Ronald Gregor Smith version (1957 rev.)[7] and the more recent translation by Walter Kaufmann (1970). Both are important in different ways. I do, however, use "mutuality" (Smith) as the preferred translation for *Gegenseitigkeit* in most cases, rather than "reciprocity" (Kaufmann) since the latter seems to me to have contractual or bargaining connotations in many contexts which are at variance with the sense of Buber's fundamental statement.

I also use "I-Thou" (Smith) as the preferred translation for "Ich-Du," rather than "I-You" (Kaufmann). The issue here is more complex. Neither term is without it problematic features as a way of rendering in contemporary English the subtleties of Buber's thought. Kaufmann regards "thou" as inappropriate because it sounds "religious" or "theological," and its use in this context would mislead the reader into supposing that Buber's book is basically a work in religion or theology, conventionally understood. Kaufmann regards "thou" as both the sign and the road by means of which an alien Protestant piety has been imported into the thoroughly Jewish world of *Ich und Du.*[8] There is no gainsaying the fact that "you" is the better term with respect to its ability to suggest ordinariness. That is not unimportant, since Buber is interested in dealing with the ordinary, quotidian world, not the religious or sacred as opposed to the secular or profane. "Thou" is heard by some as giving the book an overtly religious tone or a mystical dimension. To that extent "you" is preferable, and its use could well help to demystify and to detheologize the impression which the use of "thou" in the book might convey. On the other hand, "you" is also used in contemporary English in two ways that complicate and which call into question its appropriateness as a vehicle for Buber's intention.

(1) "You" is both nominative and objective in form. "Thou" is

only used in the nominative (''thee'' is the objective form), and hence is a better metaphor for the nonobjectifying attitude of mutuality. ''Thou'' also is not infrequently used to express the kind of intimacy Buber seems to have in mind, an intimacy which Kaufmann feels is expressed only in ''you.''
(2) In addition, ''you'' is both singular and plural in usage. ''Thou'' is inescapably singular, and hence is more suitable for the word of relation which one can speak only to one other. Few commentators on Buber's work, even those who find Kaufmann's translation correcting in several places, invigorating, and fresh, follow him in his subsitution of ''you'' for ''thou.'' Each translation has its inadequacies, but ''I-Thou'' seems, on balance, to be less misleading.

I want to record my gratitude for the extraordinary hospitality accorded me by the Hebrew University of Jerusalem in the winter and spring of 1974, when some of the research for the present work was begun, and especially by Mrs. Margot Cohn, the curator of the Martin Buber Archives. Special thanks are also due the Colgate University Research Council which aided the research and manuscript preparation. One chapter of this work is a considerably revised version of an essay published earlier. I use that material here with permission of the original publisher, whose cooperation I am happy to acknowledge: *The Journal of Ecumenical Studies,* for permission to reprint ''Buber's view of Jesus as Brother'' (Vol. 14, No. 2, Spring 1972, pp. 203—218). Some of the material in Chapter IV appeared in my article ''Mutuality in Jerusalem,'' published in *Religion in Life,* Autumn 1975, Abingdon Press, whose permission I hereby acknowledge. The many students who have shared my course on Martin Buber over the years have contributed in ways that can no longer be identified, but which some of them may nonetheless recognize. My wife, Wanda Warren Berry, and our daughters Martha and Ruth were together with me in Jerusalem where this project was born. They are the three women in my life from whom I have learned what it means for one person to speak ''Thou'' to another. In this work I am but speaking ''Thou'' in return.

I. The Tree

That living wholeness and unity of the tree, which denies itself to the sharpest glance of the mere investigator and discloses itself to the glance of one who says Thou, *is there when he, the sayer of* Thou, *is there: it is he who vouchsafes to the tree that it manifest this unity and wholeness; and now the tree which is in being manifests them.*

—Martin Buber, *I and Thou.*

Ich betrachte einen Baum.[1] ("I consider a tree.") For many people those words call into question the project for the personalization of modern life to which Martin Buber invites us in the opening paragraphs of *I and Thou*. That his vision of mutuality might help heal the sickness in our relationships with one another is quickly recognized. But the consequence of such a vision for our relation with the natural, with the tree, seems puzzling and contradictory. Many readers find the concern with nature so to border on magic or mysticism that they think it can appropriately be ignored. Although it might not seriously disqualify Buber's invitation to reciprocity, they regard the call to "consider a tree" as a curious idiosyncrasy or an embarrassing romantic whimsy. Thus the connection of Buber's vision of mutuality to the natural, to the tree, has remained unidentified and undeveloped, or forgotten altogether. I hope here to correct this misfortune, and to show how Buber's contemplation of the tree points to an absolutely central dimension of his whole program.

The distinguishing feature of Buber's philosophy is his insistence that what he calls "the innateness of the longing for relation"[2] is not expressed in the sphere of the inter-human alone. This consideration should be enough to alert us to the likelihood that Buber intends something different from the program of other philosophers of this century concerned with the social character of an existence that is fully human (Marcel, Mead). A view of the coming-to-be-of-human-life that insists on its possibility in relation to our life with nature and our life with aesthetic forms[3] has something quite distinctive to suggest about what it means to exist humanly. That Buber identifies three spheres of relation is, of course, well known. But the nonhuman, particularly the sphere of nature, has never been much attended to either by Buber or his interpreters. "The centrality of human relationships" is so plainly Buber's emphasis, that, as Walter Kaufmann reported, "critics have actually noted with surprise and protested with complete incomprehension that there should be any mention at all of a tree and of a cat" in his foundational work *I and Thou*.[4] In addressing a cat or tree as "thou" Buber is charged, by Bryan Fair, with "indulging in the pathetic fallacy."[5] And Will Herberg thought the criticism of mysticizing so often brought against Buber was "not altogether unmerited."[6]

Yet even Professor Kaufmann does not mention the sphere of nature again in his provocative prologue, nor does he do anything to diminish the surprise. The editors of the Buber volume of the *Library of Living Philosophers* judged that its thirty essays represented "a wide range of fields that does justice to most aspects of Martin Buber's thought. The only notable omission," they thought, "is social philosophy."[7] Yet there is no essay devoted to a discussion of nature, as there is of art. Nevertheless, Charles Hartshorne does propose some interpretive clues in his essay on "Martin Buber's Metaphysics";[8] and although Nathan Rotenstreich recognized that human life is lived not just with other human beings but with the whole created world, he insisted that "the phenomenon of 'dialogical life' is not only the constant theme in Buber's thought but also his main contribution to what might prima facie be called an ontology of human life."[9]

Michael Wyschogrod's excellent entry on Martin Buber in *The Encyclopedia of Philosophy* notes that the I-Thou and I-It distinction is not interchangeable with that between the I-person and I-thing, since "a person as well as an inanimate thing can be viewed as a thing, or in Buber's terminology, an 'It.'"[10] But he makes nothing of this observation and concentrates on the inter-human. In his appreciative summary of the four major legacies of Buber's thought, published not long after Buber's death, Eugene Borowitz points to nothing on nature.[11]

Of those who have treated either relevant texts in depth or Buber's thought comprehensively, only a few have considered Buber's discussion of nature sympathetically and found it to be a relevant and appropriate dimension of his vision. In his still definitive consideration of *Martin Buber: The Life of Dialogue*, Maurice Friedman recognizes the integrity of Buber's threefold world of relation,[12] and is thus able to treat approvingly the early material in *Daniel*.[13] Robert Wood develops an affirmative clarification of the subject in his detailed examination of ontological issues in *I and Thou*.[14] Wood pays special heed to the way in which "meeting with the subhuman exercised a deep influence upon Martin Buber,"[15] and collects several of the major references to the natural world. The positive evaluations of Friedman and Wood provide the clues which this chapter seeks to follow out.

Much of Buber's effort was obviously centered on identifying the possibilities between persons, but all interpreters agree that he sought to develop a perspective that might be taken toward all that meets us in any way whatever. Of the two nonhuman spheres of relation Buber himself has written in some detail about art,[16] including the theater,[17] and the secondary literature on aesthetic implications of Buber's thought is having a steady if modest growth. He was not silent, of course, about nature: he announced the basis for the sphere of the nature; identified some aspects of its problematic; referred to rocks, plants, and animals in a variety of ways; provided some signals for its development, but did not follow them out systematically or attempt to "pull it all together," as it were.

Buber frequently called attention to his enthusiasm for the concrete: "Early I foresaw that . . . no matter how I resisted, I was inescapably destined to love the world."[18] That love for "the grace that appears ever anew in earthly material"[19] was destined to remain what Buber called a "remarkable frontier area,"[20] one which he was not able to explore in depth. He proclaimed a charter for this care of "the holy treasure of our actuality,"[21] but realized that it was not given to him to pursue the subject of the natural sphere any further. The need of the hour was for serious work on the interhuman; that took Buber's energies and life's devotion. The disappearance of personal life in the modern world called him to speak for the personal. It is remarkable that when he spoke about the turning of one person to another, he exposed an attitude with which the crisis that had come over the world could be countered: "... the fate of man will depend on whether the rehallowing of existence takes place," he wrote.[22] The demand of the historical hour for Buber was to do the "rehallowing" work with respect to the interhuman. But the demand of the present historical moment prompts us to pick up Buber's intimations and to suggest how they might assist in the "rehallowing" work with respect to the sphere of nature. It may be given to our time, when ecological consciousness has been increasingly raised, to identify the programmatic issues of the natural, and to outline the manner in which the way of dialogue can sanction a responsible care for the earth needed now with urgency.

Our reflection on Buber's view of nature begins with an analysis of those passages in which Buber actually refers to some natural thing or being, and those passages in which Buber advances some clues for an uncovering of his fundamental principles, although not every mention or appearance of the word "nature" is itself useful. Our intent is to identify all those references and word usages of the sphere of nature that something is made of, omitting, however, all references to the things and beings of the natural world that appear in Buber's always illuminating discussions of biblical passages.[23]

Buber refers to the four Empodoclean elements: Earth (mica, a heap of stones, a clump of earth, a sandy plain, a desert); air (the breeze, and a gust of air in an organ's pipes); fire (the sun); and water (a lake, the sea, with its tides and waves).

Botanical entities include: flowers, fruit (and wine), a garden, grain of sand, grass, madrepores, mushrooms, thistle, and trees of several species—an unspecified tree, linden or lime, oak, olive, stone pine, and one that is simply planted in the earth.

Zoological entities include: beaver, a bird, butterfly and its chrysalis, a cat, cricket, a dog, horse, lion cub, monkeys, swallows, tuna.

A. That listing already trades on the schema which Buber himself included in his "Postscript" or "Afterword" to the second edition of *I and Thou* (1957).[24] This classification is built upon the metaphorical use of the concept of "threshold." The concern is not simple proximity in spatial terms to the realm of our life with one another and all of its dialogic possibilities—that would be "threshold" in a more literal usage. Buber means by "threshold," rather, the positive significance or value of such nearness to the mutuality or reciprocity that is possible when both partners of the relation are human beings. In this schema the elements (earth/rocks, air, fire/sun, and water) are "sub-threshold"; botanical entities are "pre-threshold"; and zoological entities are at the "threshold" of mutuality. The full import of this schema will be clearer after an elucidation of other modes of classification has been undertaken.

B. The variety of Buber's nature references seems to be illuminated more by a classifying mode based on their function, the purpose which they seem intended to serve in Buber's writing, even if it is not always easy in some cases to see clearly what the primary function is. Four such different purposes are being served by these references to the sphere of nature.

(1) One group of usages is clearly neutral with respect to the main features of Buber's program. Among such references are some aspects of Buber's recurring dream in which a lion cub tears away the flesh from his arm.[25] Although this original remembrance of a cry upon awaking and a more distanced cry heard in response launched Buber's discussion of soundless communication, the lion cub has only the existence of a dream's certitude, and is at most catalytic of reflection, without positive

value in itself. Included here as well are items of his employment of nature words solely or primarily as figures of speech,
whose appearance points only to the worldly dimension of
Buber's literary imagination, and tells us nothing as such about
his view of nature. For example:

> If I were a bird, says the faithful man, then I would not have life in my
> belly but in my wings, and not in my balancing but in my soaring.[26]

> . . . the one thing that is needful . . . came to me mute and concealed,
> like the grain of seed in the earth; it laid itself on my breast and
> remained with me.[27]

> I perceive, as the member of settlement of madrepores may perceive,
> with the organs of the community . . .[28]

> The trees condemn him who is not upright and attentive; the flowers
> judge him who does not open himself and submit himself to the sun;
> and he who does not know the peace of becoming, against him every
> blade of grass raises itself like a flaming sword.[29]

(2) A more revealing group of images are references to or
quotations from other writers. Commentators sometimes con-
fuse these usages as being original with Buber, and in some
cases Buber has so appropriated the others' figures as to make
them almost his own. But even if these are not original with
Buber, his use of or comments about them disclose something of
his own sense of the natural.

> (Buber quotes Boehme); "Whenever I pick up and look at a stone or
> clump of earth, I see the Above and the Below, indeed the whole
> world therein, only in such a way that in each of these things some
> particular property is greatest, according to which it is named."[30]

But, as Buber notes, Boehme's concern always seems to be to
make an application to human life. This should not surprise us
since "in the human being," so Buber cites Boehme, "the
whole creation lies; even heaven and earth with all beings,"
even the very being of God.[31] Buber continues: "This

marvelous world-feeling (*Weltgefühl*) has become completely our own. We have woven it into our inmost experience.'' And then in words that seem explicitly to resonate with eucharistic language, shorn of their historicality, Buber adds:

> Whenever I guide a piece of fruit to my mouth, I feel: this is my body; and whenever I place wine to my lip, I feel: this is my blood.

> And sometimes there comes to us the desire to put our arms around a young tree, and to feel the same surge of life as in ourselves, or to read the secret of our own life in the eyes of a dumb animal. We experience the travels and fading of the most distant stars as something which happens to us. There are even moments in which our organism is quite completely another piece of nature.

> But if for Boehme everything is in the human being, any development is only an unfolding, Everything grows from the inside out. We recognize the world, since we have it in us. . . . So, for Boehme, everything is in everything; he knows no differing value among things.

> ''The sun,'' as Boehme says, gives itself with its power without distinction; it loves each fruit and vegetable and withholds itself from no thing; it wants only that from each cabbage, or whatever it is, a good fruit will be drawn. . . .''32

But this is not ordinary sacramental language, in which concrete, particular actualities of our earthly-historical form of existence are regarded as being endowed with extraordinary meaning, with being transignified. This way of envisioning the unity of the individual and the world seems, in fact, to merge the two altogether, so that in the end whatever distinctions are to be made, will all be within the context of a harmony inseparable into its component units. For Boehme, according to Buber, ''the world is a harmony of individuals.'' The tones which their individuality unfolds is like the harmony which an organ makes:

> . . . an organ of many voices will be empowered by a single draft of air, which gives to each its voice, indeed in each pipe its tone, and is still

only a single draft of air in all the voices, which in each voice sounds
according to the way the instrument or organ is made.[33]

There remains, nonetheless, a fundamental ambiguity in Buber's playing with Boehme's images. He approves of Boehme's
longing for a deeper unity than that which can be provided
by the two forces which move through all existence—the
longing for conflict and the longing of love. These longings are
bridges between the I and the world.

> Conflict is a bridge since in and through it the I develops and reveals
> itself in its beauty to another I; and love is a bridge since in it being
> unites itself with God. Out of the mixture of the two comes life, in
> which things neither exist in rigid separation, nor melt into one
> another, but reciprocally condition themselves.[34]

In this very early piece Buber indentifies with Boehme over
against Feuerbach, since unity for the latter is founded on the
difference between the I and Thou; and Buber sees himself as
standing even nearer to St. Francis who called the trees, the
birds, and the stars his brothers, sisters; and still nearer to the
Vedanta. Yet in this whole discussion of Boehme's images, and
the contrasts with Feuerbach, Buber resists the obliteration of
the division of the I from the world, and does not think of himself
as succumbing to the alchemical presuppositions of Boehme's
view of the world.[35]

Buber's very early conceptualizing of the unity of the I and
the world is developed as he works with and thus displays
nearness to and distance from these images from Boehme. After
the maturing of his thought into an appreciation of the necessity
of the absolute distinction between the self and the other, the
image of unity is displaced by the image of relation. This is
especially clear in his comments on the landscape painting of
Leopold Krakauer. Here there is the perception of the artist's
treatment of the thistle, the olive tree, even a heap of stones. But
now, instead of lauding a vision in which some of the distinctiveness of these actualities is obscured or at least dimmed, Buber
now insists on the indispensability of the distinction between

face-to-face being and the so-called passive object. He admires
Krakauer's work because in his landscapes Buber finds that
"Nature too moves towards us, even in the most extreme
motionlessness; it has to do with us."[36]

> The inner tension that works out of the restless and yet so finished
> form of the thistle, the great inner trembling that is frozen into the
> limbs of the olive tree as the life pain of a man into the lines of his face,
> yes, even the immeasurable movement of the smallest little part that
> hides behind the apparent deadness of a heap of stones but that lets
> something like a strange knocking penetrate from itself to us.[37]

Krakauer was important for Buber since he gave testimony to
the genuine meeting of the I and the natural, not their identity.

(3) A third group of images functions to illustrate one or
another of the irreducible elements of relation—especially the
particularity and the presence of the other. These are not facts of
the objective situations as such, but rather are basic movements
which bring about the essential relation. The movements are
twofold: the primal setting at a distance, and the entering into
relation. Although there is no inclusion, no mutual confirmation
in any of these examples, there is a genuine illustration of the
over-againstness and the openness of the other to relation. The
tree that he contemplated in *I and Thou* is discrete and available,
but not a being with which one identifies one's own being
through the embracing, as in the Boehme essay. Even as the
tree is known-in-relation it remains unknown in its nonobjectifi-
cation. That much, in itself, is suggestive of a continuing aspect
of the relational possibilities in the sphere of the interhuman.
The overall significance of his several tree references, however,
has to do more with clarifying the difference between the human
and the subhuman, and will be discussed below. The autobio-
graphical references to a horse, and a cat, and another to a child
and its dog, while illustrating the same contrast, do, as well,
serve to exemplify something about mutuality.

First the horse.

> When I was eleven years of age, spending the summer on my grand-
> parents' estate, I used, as often as I could do it unobserved, to steal

into the stable and gently stroke the neck of my darling, a broad dapple-grey horse. It was not a casual delight but a great certainly friendly, but also deeply stirring happening. If I am to explain it now, beginning from the still very fresh memory of my hand, I must say that what I experienced in touch with the animal was the Other, the immense otherness of the Other, which, however, did not remain strange like the otherness of the ox and the ram, but rather let me draw near and touch it. When I stroked the mighty mane, sometimes marvellously smooth-combed, at other times just as astonishingly wild, and felt the life beneath my hand, it was as though the element of vitality itself bordered on my skin, something that was not I, was certainly not akin to me, palpably the other, not just another, really the Other itself; and yet it let me approach, confided itself to me, placed itself elementally in the relation of *Thou* and *Thou* with me. The horse, even when I had not begun by pouring oats for him into the manger, very gently raised his massive head, ears flicking, then snorted quietly, as a conspirator given a signal meant to be recognizable only by his fellow-conspirator; and I was approved. But once—I do not know what came over the child, at any rate it was childlike enough—it struck me about the stroking, what fun it gave me, and suddenly I became conscious of my hand. The game went on as before, but something had changed, it was no longer the same thing. And the next day, after giving him a rich feed, when I stroked my friend's head he did not raise his head. A few years later, when I thought back to the incident, I no longer supposed that the animal had noticed my defection. But at the time I considered myself judged.38

Notice the preservation of the otherness of the horse, all the while Buber speaks of the relation, which, while not fully reciprocal, is so strongly present that it can be described only by granting the horse both an initiatory power ("the horse, even when I had not begun by pouring oats for him into the manger. . . snorted quietly, as a conspirator gives a signal meant to be recognizable only by his fellow-conspirators") and a responsive agency ("let me draw near and touch it."). In that relation the young Buber knew himself "approved," and such a confirming act is one of the gifts of relation.

Second, the cat.

I sometimes look into the eyes of a house cat. The domesticated animal has not by any means received the gift of the truly "eloquent" glance from *us,* as a human conceit suggests sometimes; what it has from us is only the ability—purchased with the loss of its elementary naturalness—to turn this glance upon us brutes. In this process some mixture of surprise and question has come into it, into its dawn and even its rise—and this was surely wholly absent from the original glance, for all its anxiety. Undeniably, this cat began its glance by asking me with a glance that was ignited by the breath of my glance: "Can it be that you mean me? Do you actually want that I should not merely do tricks for you? Do I concern you? Am I there for you? Am I there? What is that coming from you? What is that around me? What is it about me? What is that?!" ("I" is here a paraphrase of a word of I-less self-reference that we lack. "That" represents the flood of man's glance in the entire actuality of its power to relate.) There the glance of the animal, the language of anxiety, had risen hugely—and set almost at once. My glance, to be sure, endured longer; but it no longer retained the flood of man's glance.[39]

Notice the emphasis on the eyes, the glance, as a medium for relation, so close upon the threshold of mutuality that Buber is constrained to characterize the meaning of the glance in terms of eloquence, that is, in terms of speech from the I (the cat) to the Thou (Buber himself) ("Can it be that you mean me? . . . ."). But the "I" in this case is used metaphorically, "a paraphrase of a word of I-less self-reference that we lack."[40] In the animal references the eye is the organ of relation which is more like than unlike the way the eye works in the interhuman sphere. Although the "creatures stir across from us," they remain, as Buber put it in *I and Thou,* "unable to come to us.[41] Yet these brief animal narratives indicate that Buber wanted to hold out for something very much like that very "coming to us."

The eyes of an animal have the capacity of a great language. Independent, without any need of the assistance of sounds and gestures, most eloquent when they rest entirely in their glance, they express the mystery in its natural captivity, that is, in the anxiety of becoming. This state of the mystery is known only to the animal, which alone can open it up to us—for this state can only be opened up

and not revealed. The language in which this is accomplished is what
it says: anxiety—the stirring of the creature between the realms of
plantlike security and spiritual risk. This language is the stammering
of nature under the intitial grasp of spirit, before language yields to
spirit's cosmic risk which we call man. But no speech will ever repeat
what the stammer is able to communicate. [42]

With the account of the child and its dog we see combined
the concern for particularity and the power of the glance.

> The experience from which I have proceeded and ever again
> proceed is simply this, that one meets another. Another, that does not
> mean, for example, a ''dog,'' an ''English sheep dog,'' one that is to
> be described thus-and-thus, but this particular animal, which a child
> once, about to run by him, looked in the eyes and remained standing,
> they both remained standing while the child laid his hand on the head
> of the dog and called him by a name that he had just invented or found.
> When later at home he sought to make clear to himself what had been
> special about the animal, he managed without concepts; he only
> needed them when he had to relate the occurrence to his best friend. [43]

Notice here a third aspect of relation exemplified, namely, the
irrelevance and absence of both any concepts and also any
possible use for or surrender to conceptual activity of any sort.
The child needed no concepts in the clarification of his own
awareness of the remembered mutuality with the dog. Concepts
were required only for communicating, for telling the story of his
encounter with the dog to a friend. In such a task conceptuality is
indispensable, but it must be seen through. That is, one must
be open, in speaking and in silence, to the "abyss beneath the
concepts," which makes possible "rational intercourse with
that which is beyond concepts." [44]
  In each of these three human-animal episodes the ontological unconditionality of the otherness of the other is preserved, while the essential presence of the other as other is affirmed.
The horse, the cat, and the dog are able to regard the human
person in a speaking sort of way, announcing themselves, as it
were. As the two beings move toward each other, they become
present, each to the other, not as objects, but as partners. Each

retains his/its full independence, but fully mutual confirmation is lacking.

> A being to whom I really say "Thou" is not for me in this moment my object, about whom I observe this and that or whom I put to this or that use, but my partner who stands over against me in his own right and existence and yet related to me in his life.[45]

The dialogical principle, thus, will call into question every "self-sufficient principle of existence" in the name of a partnership, a co-being, of one with another for which animals are always possible candidates in a special way because of the spontaneity which they share with us.[46] "I find," Buber said, ". . . that our relationship to the domestic animals with whom we live, and even that to the plants in our garden, is properly included as the lowest floor of the ethical building."[47] This is possible because, within the limits of the latency of their two-foldness, animals can indeed turn toward another, including us if we are present to them. This movement is more discernible with domesticated animals, but it is not exclusive with nor confined to those whom we have tamed.

> Man draws animals into his own sphere and moves them to accept him, a stranger, in an elementary manner and to accede to his ways. He obtains from them an often astonishing active response to his approach, to his address—and on the whole this response is the stronger and more direct, the more his relation amounts to a genuine You-saying. Not infrequently animals, like children, see through feigned tenderness. But outside the tamed circle, too, we occasionally enounter a similar contact between men and animals: some men have deep down in their being a potential partnership with animals—most often persons who are by no means "animalic" by nature but rather spiritual.[48]

If we are to judge by the animal episodes, the limits of relation are simply the limits of awareness. "No kind of appearance or event is fundamentally excluded from the series of the things through which from time to time something is said to me. Nothing can refuse to be the vessel for the Word."[49]

Because he believed this to be so, Buber was able to "welcome every philosophy of existence that leaves open the door leading to otherness,"[50] although none opens it far enough, or at least as far as the philosophy of relation of which Buber has been giving an account.

(4) A fourth group of images functions to clarify the possibilities for the interhuman by way of contrast with the subhuman. The illustrations here are primarily of rocks (more specifically mica), and trees, of several kinds, and a few additional animal references.

(C. We must indicate parenthetically in order to employ it here, another way of classifying Buber's nature references, intimated in the discussion of Krakauer above. This third way organizes the passages with respect to their connection to the maturity of Buber's dialogical philosophy. We distinguish, therefore, those that come from the early Buber from those which come from the later Buber. By 'early' we mean before the discovery of mutuality, when Buber was deeply involved in, influenced by, and yet moving away from several philosophies of unity/unification; by 'later' we mean *I and Thou* [1923] and afterwards when Buber was ever again working out the implications of his most fundamental insight—the twofoldness of the human way of being in and being with respect to the world. It is necessary to utilize this distinction here because the references which clarify the difference between human and subhuman relational possibilities are often to the same subhuman entities, references to which appear in both the early and later Buber material. So at this point two sets of distinctions will need to be kept in mind: the function to clarify the human-subhuman contrast, and the early-later placing.)

Even more than at other places it is important to heed here Buber's own caution and avoid speaking of nature in general and attend, rather, to the possibilities and limitations of mutuality that are open to particular beings and things in their discreteness.

Almost all of the references to the elements, even the neutral passages, appear in the early Buber, and suggest how deeply he was influenced by aspects of the German nature-mysticism of the time. Bodies of water appear in the quasi-auto-biographical *Daniel,* particularly in the fifth dialogue: "On Unity: Dialogue by the Sea." Notice the twofold status of the lake or the sea: the water is a sign to me of my belonging, of my sense of being home in the world. But more than a sign: it is a source from which I have sprung and to which I shall return; it is home; it is mother; it is; after Empedocles, that which is nearest my true self.

Lukas: I had spoken to him in the evening. Rather, he had spoken to me. He stood by the sea, which was autumnal green and white as today, and looked with a still more tender gaze than usual at the water. Then he said: "Now the mother is free and no longer the maid of sun and heaven and may bear freely her own colors." You must know, Daniel, that he never called the sea anything else than the mother.[51]

From day to day the question mounts higher in me, what sort of a sea is it on which we travel, they and I, what sort of a sea has given birth to us, them and me. I know that in some way I am myself this sea, but I cannot reach there where I am it. And yet Elias reached there. Is what we call death, therefore, perhaps the way?[52]

Elias knelt on the edge of the bark, bent over, his arms extended perpendicular to the water; his two hands stroked it ever again like the limbs of a beloved being. Kajetan said to me that he had to think of Empedocles at that moment; with such movement of the hands he had always imagined Empedocles. That struck him so that he had to look away. When he looked again, Elias was no longer in the bark. Kajetan tore open the window, shouted something to the people below, which they did not understand, and ran down the stairs. It did not take long to send out a boat, but it took very long until they found the corpse. They tried in vain to awaken life in him.[53]

One morning I had climbed a small Alp from which one looked down on an equally small lake enclosed by crags. This lake received my whole gaze and held it like a magic crystal. Soon the surrendered gaze was freighted with my forces and my movement. Relaxing I felt how everything in me went into it; it grew as I waned; and finally even the living power of grief, my orphaned state, went out of me—I was as little orphaned now as a newborn child whose mother has died. Thus I fell asleep. I still knew my glance to be hovering over the deep, then this too disappeared before the consuming nothingness. I slept in the timeless while the happening of the world meted out my hours.[54]

Yet for all the power of the sea, for all the lake's reception of my active gaze, it cannot say "Thou" to me; it cannot step, in its overagainstness, into relation with me.

Buber was dismayed with the restriction of a subject-object epistemology, and sought throughout his life to develop an approach more hospitable to the linkage he saw between human beings and the world. That dichotomy was overcome in the "oneness" of his Boehme essay, and the overcoming appears in *Daniel* with the language of "unity."

> On a gloomy morning I walked upon the highway, saw a piece of mica lying, lifted it up and looked at it for a long time; the day was no longer gloomy, so much light was caught in the stone. And suddenly as I raised my eyes from it, I realized that while I looked I had not been conscious of "object" and "subject"; in my looking the mica and "I" had been one; in my looking I had tasted unity. I looked at it again, the unity did not return. But there it burned in me as though to create. I closed my eyes, I gathered in strength, I bound myself with my object, I raised the mica into the kingdom of the existing. And there, Lukas, I first felt: *I*, there I first was I. The one who looked had not yet been I; only this man here, this unified man, bore the name like a crown. Now I perceived that first unity as the marble statue may perceive the block out of which it was chiseled; it was the undifferentiated, I was the unification. Still I did not understand myself; but then there flashed through me the memory; thus had my body fifteen human years before done the simple deed and, the fingers entwined, united life and death to "I."[55]

The limitation of that interpretation is exposed in *I and Thou*, when Buber reaches for a new way to understand that contact with a piece of mica that would be congruent with his philosophy of relation. The missing ingredient in his earlier conceptuality was the "between," that is, each other's distinctness, or particularity.

There is so much that can never break through the crust of thinghood! O fragment of mica, it was while contemplating you that I first understood that I is not something "in me" — yet I was associated with you only in myself; it was only in me, not between you and me that it happened that time. But when something does emerge from among things, something living, and becomes a being for me, and comes to me, near and eloquent, how unavoidably briefly it is for me nothing but You! It is not the relationship that necessarily wanes, but the actuality of its directness. Love itself cannot abide in a direct relation; it endures, but in the alternation of actuality and latency. Every You in the world is compelled by its nature to become a thing for us or at least to enter again and again and again into thinghood.[56]

Buber liked trees. The tree he considered in *I and Thou* had many predecessors and successors; sometimes it is simply "a tree," or "this tree"; other times it is a pine, an oak, a linden tree. The trees in the early Buber are embraced; the person feels at one with the tree, or at one with life that surges through the tree.

After a descent during which I had to utilize without a halt the late light of a dying day, I stood on the edge of a meadow, now sure of the safe way, and let the twilight come down upon me. Not needing a support and yet willing to accord my lingering a fixed point, pressed my stick against a trunk of an oak tree. Then I felt in twofold fashion my contact with being; here, where I held the stick, and there, where it touched the bark. Appearing to be only where I was, I nonetheless found myself there, too, where I found the tree.

At that time dialogue appeared to me. For the speech of man, wherever it is genuine speech, is like that stick; that means: truly directed address. Here, where I am, where ganglia and organs of speech help me to form and to send forth the word, here I "mean" him to whom I send it, I intend him, this one unexchangeable man. But also there, where he is, something of me is delegated, something that is not all substantial in nature like that being-here, rather pure vibration and incomprehensible; that remains there, with him, the man meant by me, and takes part in the receiving of my word. I encompass him to whom I turn.[57]

The dialogue which appeared here is truly directed address, but without any response as such. The twofoldness here is the self and the tree, both of which are found when the walking stick is pressed against the trunk of the tree. But the tree is not bodied over against the self. Contact is made, but it is more with being than with the oak tree in its uniqueness. That sense of things appears with the stone pine, the presentation of which clearly anticipates the 1923 tree.

> Look at this stone pine. You may compare its properties with those of other stone pines, other trees, other plants, establish what it has in common, explore what it is composed of and how it grew. That will be useful to you in the useful auxiliary world of names and classifications, of reports about how things arose and how they evolved. You experience nothing of the truth of this being. And now seek to draw near to this stone pine itself. Not with the power of the feeling glance alone—that can present you only with the fullness of an image: much, but not all. Rather, with all your direct power, receive the tree, surrender yourself to it. Until you feel its bark as your skin and the springing forth of a branch from the trunk like the striving in your muscles; until your feet cleave and grope like roots and your skull arches itself like a light-heavy crown; until you recognize your children in the soft blue cones; yes, truly until you are transformed. But also in the transformation your direction is with you, and through it you experience the tree so that you attain in it to the unity. For it draws you back into yourself; the transformation clears away like a fog; and around your direction a being forms itself, the tree, so that you experience its unity, the unity. Already it is transplanted out of the earth of space into the earth of the soul, already it tells its secret to your heart, already you perceive the mystery of the real. Was it not a tree among trees? But now it has become the tree of eternal life.[58]

But note that here Buber is still working with language that does not sufficiently safeguard the discreteness of all beings: one needs to feel the bark of the tree as one's own skin. This being with, but being 'too close' to, the tree is eventually transformed in the power of an image that is open to the real otherness of the tree.

> But it can also happen, if will and grace are joined, that as I contemplate the tree I am drawn into a relation, and the tree ceases to be

an It. The power of exclusiveness has seized me.

This does not require me to forego any of the modes of contemplation. There is nothing that I must not see in order to see, and there is no knowledge that I must forget. Rather is everything, picture and movement, species and instance, law and number included and inseparably fused.

Whatever belongs to the tree is included: its form and its mechanics, its color and its chemistry, its conversation with the elements and its conversation with the stars—all this in its entirety.

The tree is no impression, no play of my imagination, no aspect of a mood; it confronts me bodily and has to deal with me as I must deal with it—only differently.

One should not try to dilute the meaning of the relation; relation is reciprocity.

Does the tree then have consciousness, similar to our own? I have no experience of that. But thinking that you have brought this off in your own case, must you again divide the indivisible? What I encounter is neither the soul of a tree nor a dryad, but the tree itself.[59]

Notice here that "being at one with" has been replaced by a "relation," in which the tree "has to deal with me as I must deal with it—only differently." But a basic feature of reciprocity/mutuality has now begun to appear for the first time with sufficient clarity in the tree episodes—the feature of wholeness, in addition to mutual particularity. A third aspect of relation that is supremely present in the interhuman sphere, but is adumbrated with the trees, is the feature of 'purposelessness.''

> The man who gazes without purpose on a tree is no less ''everyday''
> than the one who looks at a tree to learn which branch would make the
> best stick. The first way of looking belongs to the constitution of the
> ''everyday'' no less than the second.[60]

The gratuitous character of relation is its unaccountability, its mystery, its nonutility. This purposelessness is the immediate implication of letting the other be in its wholeness and its distance (what I have been calling its particularity or distinctness). I move toward the other, but I can will only to let it be itself; otherwise I seek to assimilate it to my world, and in that act relation is destroyed.

An ancient linden tree once stood on the path that I took time after time. I always accepted it as it was given to me, and that was enough for me. . . . I accepted the thing or unthing, which had become propertyless and uncanny, the thing that had waited for me in order to become once again the blooming and fragrant linden of my sense world. I said to the sense-deprived linden-*x* what Goethe said to the fully sensible rose: 'So it is you.'[61]

That "standing in relation to a tree" of which Buber speaks is not so 'mystical' or so 'peculiar' an event, and certainly not an imprisoning one, is suggested by Nan Hirleman's story of a sunset in the woods.[62] She had walked, largely in silence, with a friend, who had suggested that the search for depth experiences might deflect one from an appreciation of the detail at hand. "To really see that tree over there with the sun on its leaves," her friend had remarked, "is not to go down deep into the essence of the leaf, but simply to see the way the sun makes that leaf translucent . . . and to look at all the different colors of green the sun expresses in these leaves." But Nan Hirleman knew that she "was trying so hard to 'get into' the experience, that all the leaves looked pretty much the same . . ." to her. But with the suggestive insight of his words, she concludes, "I looked again and saw the leaves with new vision."

They weren't just leaves; there were separate leaves that were translucent in the sun, and that translucence was punctuated only by the veins of the leaf. And then, to my dismay, I caught myself trying to 'get into the leaf' and have an experience with the leaf, instead of simply noticing the details of it.[63]

This openness to present detail, before the dismaying movement of trying to make a connection with the leaves, is, I think, the "quiet, devoted relationship to nearby life" of which Buber speaks. He calls for us to attend to the particularity of whatever it is that is over against us in its particularity if the fulness of life is ever to be known. As Nan Hirleman "learned" from her friend, so in such a way one learns from Buber's report, "I consider a tree," and lives out the prompting of another teacher ın Israel who said "Consider the lilies. . . ."

In the previous section we identified some paragraphs in which animal references functioned to illustrate one or another dimension of mutuality. In this section I want briefly to identify some remaining animal references which function primarily to illustrate the contrast between the possibilities for relation in the human and subhuman spheres.

> The It is the chrysalis, the You the butterfly. Only it is not always as if these states took turns so neatly; often it is an intricately entangled series of events that is tortuously dual.[64]

> Every actual relationship in the world alternates between actuality and latency; every individual You must disappear into the chrysalis of the It in order to grow wings again. In the pure relationship, however, latency is merely actuality drawing a deep breath during which the You remains present.[65]

The chrysalis-butterfly image provides an analogue in the subhuman sphere to the exalted melancholy of our human lot. The alternation between actuality and latency suggests the inevitability which prevents every relation from being preserved in space and time. Our lot is melancholy since the relation cannot be sustained, but exalted, nonetheless, since it can emerge ever again from the realm of objectification into that of relation.

The remaining animal references illustrate interhuman possibilities by way of contrast with the subhuman. "An animal's actions are concerned with its future and the future of its young, but only man imagines the future."[66] For this reason

> ... the beaver's dam is extended in a time-realm, but the planted tree is rooted in the world of time, and he who plants the first tree is he who will expect the Messiah.[67]

Yet an "animal does not know the state of relation because one cannot stand in a relation to something that is not perceived as contrasted and existing for itself."[68] A monkey can use a stone to crack nuts, for example; but it is not able sufficiently to imagine the future so as to put the stone aside to use again tomorrow for the same purpose.

> Only man, as man, gives distance to things which he comes upon in his realm; he sets them in their independence as things which from now on continue to exist ready for a function and which he can make wait for him so that on each occasion he may master them again, and bring them into action. . . . A monkey can swing the branch of a tree as a weapon; but man alone is capable of providing the branch with a separate existence . . .[69]

Although the animal has objects even as does humankind, the animal has only objects. Man alone "has face-to-face being."[70] Because of this Buber concludes that animals indeed have an environment but cannot properly be said to have a world.

> For by "world" we must mean that which is extended substantially beyond the realm of the observer who is *in* the world and as such is independent. . . . An animal's organism gathers . . . the elements which meet the necessities and wants of its life. . . . [But] it is only man who replaces this unsteady conglomeration . . . by a unity which can be imagined or thought by him as existing for itself. . . . Only when a structure of being is independently over against a living being, an independent opposite, does a world exist.[71]

The chart which follows summarizes the data and the several modes of classification advanced so far. The sphere of nature includes the elements and both botanical and zoological entities. All of the subhuman things and beings can be grouped in accordance with their ability to respond to our presence. We are most capable of mutuality with the animals and the least possibility for mutuality, for even adverting, exists with the elements and plants. Hence Buber distinguishes them one from the other with respect to the thresholdness of their mutuality. When the examples and illustrations are grouped on these three levels, and distinguished in terms of their appearance as early or late, that is, before or after the clarification of the dialogic principle; and when this distinguishing is conjoined with identifying the examples and illustrations in terms of the four-fold set of functions (neutral or figures of speech, appropriation of language from other authors, illustrating the meaning of relation, and clarifying the possibilities for the interhuman by contrast with the subhuman) an important relationship is un-convered: the vast majority of animal references appear in the later material, and function to illustrate the meaning of mutuality. The farther one moves up from the subthreshold to the threshold of mutuality, the more completely does one leave behind the earlier material with its more frequent employment of entities with limited possibility for responding to our moving toward them. But being left behind is not being left out. Early and late Buber will insist that no thing or being, in and of itself, is necessarily excluded from being that with which I find myself in relation.

The ontological distinctiveness and the ethical import of Buber's vision of nature can be highlighted by seeing how radically it is contrasted with the world which Sartre has created in his novel *Nausea*.[72] Instead of seeing the things and beings of the world as occasions for relation in a positive sense, Antoine Roquentin finds existence at every moment distasteful and intolerable. Everything is in the way; nothing is a vehicle for meaning. The contrast is illustrated in three modes: a rock, a tree, and the eyes—paralleling Buber's mica, tree, and the glance.

First, the pebble, which assaults Roquentin, cannot alert its holder to a sense of wonder at its thinghood, let alone to any sense of oneness with it.

> Objects should not *touch* because they are not alive. You use them, put them back in place. You live among them: they are useful, nothing more. But they touch me, it is unbearable. I am afraid of being in contact with them as though they were living beasts.
>
> Now I see: I recall better what I felt the other day at the seashore when I held the pebble. It was a sort of sweetish sickness. How un-pleasant it was! It came from the stone, I'm sure of it, it passed from the stone to my hand. Yes, that's it, that's just it—a sort of nausea in the hands.[73]

Things and beings of the one world which appears twofold in accordance with our twofold attitude: the sphere of nature	The relation with the other viewed with respect to degrees or levels of mutuality/reciprocity	Examples, illustrations identified in terms of origin and function	
Zoological entities	Threshold	1 beaver—B4 2 bird—A1 3 butterfly—A3, B3 4 cat—B3 5 cricket—A1 6 dog—B3 7 horse—B3	8 lion cub—B1 9 monkey—B4 10 ox—B1 11 ram—B4 12 swallow—B4 13 tuna—B4
Botanical entities	Prethreshold	14 flowers—A1 15 fruit—A2 16 garden—A1 17 grain of seed—A1 18 grass—A1 19 madrepores—A1 20 mushrooms—A3 21 thistle—B2	22 tree—linden/lime—B3 23 tree: oak—A3 24 tree: olive—B2 25 tree: planted—B3 26 tree: stone pine—A3 27 tree—A1 28 tree—B3 29 wine—A2

The elements   Subthreshold

30 air/breeze — A1   37 desert — B1
31 air/wind — A2   38 sea — A3
32 mica — A3   39 lake — A3
33 mica — B4   40 tide — A3
34 heap of stones — A2, B2   41 waves — A3
35 clump of earth — A2   42 sun — A1
36 sandy plain — A3

It must be observed that this chart brackets out all things and beings of the natural world that appear in Buber's always illuminating discussion of biblical material.

Key: Origin: A = Early Buber—before clarification of dialogic principle
         B = Later Buber—after clarification of dialogic principle
   Functions: 1 = Neutral; figures of speech
         2 = From other authors
         3 = Illustrates meaning of relation
         4 = By contrast to clarify possiblities for the interhuman

The arabic number to the left of each illustration refers to the item in the appendix.

Second, the chestnut tree, which seized Roquentin and imprisoned him, and the glance which held him captive to the tree.

> Roquentin has been sitting on a park bench. The roots of the chestnut tree were sunk in the ground under my bench. . . . The chestnut tree pressed itself against my eyes. . . . But existence is a deflection. Everything is in the way . . . In vain I tried to count the chestnut trees, to locate them . . . The root was black and not black—playing back and forth with these words.[74]

For nearly eleven pages Sartre elaborates on the demonic fascination which Roquentin perceives the chestnut tree has birthed in him. Then, finally, when the wind shook the top of the tree and it began to move ". . . my eyes were empty and I was spell-bound by my deliverance. . . ."[75] The way in which chestnut tree compels my glance, captures me, destroys my freedom, and my humanity. The multiplicity of trees produces everywhere a sort of conspiratorial air.

How different from Buber, for whom every pebble, every tree, every animal, every thing and being of the world is a vehicle for meaning. Thus it is that Grete Schaeder can speak of Buber's "world-rejoicing existentialism."[76]

Now what are we to make of this celebration of the world's concreteness? What is the most appropriate account that can be made of Buber's move to consider a tree? The description and analysis which we have just made of representative passages in which Buber speaks of nature make it very clear that the appearance of the tree and cat in *I and Thou* is not eccentric, a matter of personal whimsy, existentialist idiosyncrasy, or a development without central relation to Buber's program. What remains to be done is to identify those moves by which we can clarify Buber's assertion of a reciprocal relation with nature. Two sorts of questions seem to be involved in making this necessary accounting.

The first of these has to do with origin. In this view to account for Buber's program with respect to nature is to locate the roots of his thought. Most of these sources are known and have been evaluated by the early and later commentators on Buber's thought: Potok, Diamond, Friedman, Kaufmann, Schaeder, and Breslauer. Such a genealogical strategy will disclose the pervasive influence of Wilhelm Dilthey's distinction between the methodology of the natural sciences (characterized by objectivity and detachment) and the methodology of the human sciences (characterized by personal participation). This approach will note Buber's dissertation treatment of Christian mysticism in the Reformation and Renaissance. It will feature Buber's continuing fascination with such authors as Jacob Boehme, Meister Eckhart, Nicholas of Cusa, whose mysticism fed Buber's worrying out a regard for the lived connection of human beings and the world. Chaim Potok, who has done some of this root charting, is sensitive to Buber's attraction to the kind of mysticism that was popular in Germany at the turn of the century, a mysticism that was less a withdrawal from and more a concern to have to do with the world in a meaningful way. Potok[77] utilizes the threefold schema originally suggested by Friedman to clarify Buber's development in working through these source materials. Buber begins with an interest in "discovering" the essential unity which already exists between human beings and their worldy environment (his essay on Boehme), moves through an approach based on the power of a fulfilled human existence to "realize" the unity of God and the world (*Daniel*), reaching finally the language of "meeting" from which Buber never departed. This way of meeting is itself worked out in Buber's discovery and appropriation of the Hasidic tradition. Hasidic religiousness, with its divine spark imagery, gave Buber a way of understanding the potential for relation which all things and beings of the world bear toward human beings. The inner meaning which Buber found Hasidic world piety to have is best expressed in the notion of "presentness," a kind of natural sacramentality by which nature is penetrated with and by holiness without being violated thereby.[78] This Hasidic orientation to religious meaning was the prism through which all Buber's earlier fascination with mysticism was refracted and given a location consistent with biblical centering on creation. As Schaeder puts it, "That the world is God's creation and that all creatures are created interrelated to one another explain the fact that a tree also could become a Thou for me. . . ."[79]

This genealogical approach that works mainly with origins does not, however fully orbed the picture becomes, exhaust the kind of accounting that needs to be given. It is one thing to see the intellectual continuities behind Buber's thought, but quite another thing to evaluate the turns his thought makes. We must ask, then, a different order of question: not what ways of seeing and symbol systems contributed to Buber's philosophy of relation (an historical task), but how can a philosophy of relation that attends to the nonhuman be justified (a philosophical and theological task), that is, rendered internally consistent and externally explanatory or at least insightful.

Most of the proposals for dealing with this task are either based on a logic which Buber himself rejected or reach a conclusion which ignores or controverts the fundamental affirmations of the life of dialogue. Charles Hartshorne has suggested, for example, that one could speak of the tree as having a soul, or as being part of an animated whole, or as being composed of animated individuals.[80] But this more sophisticated rendering of primitive animism flies in the face of Buber's repeated warning that the act of considering the tree or being bound up with the cat or dog or horse is not made possible by some hidden quality in the plant or animal. Buber's early readers may be forgiven somewhat for not taking Buber's warning with utmost seriousness, since the early Buber had not sufficiently freed himself from language and possibly from views that seemed to be mystical or nearly so. But from the second edition of *I and Thou* on only a penchant for perversity would try to force Buber into affirming what he explicitly denies. We ought to take him at his word that what he thinks that he is saying is that I do not enter into relation with the nonhuman because of its crypto-human qualities.

The by now customary explanatory model by means of which some have sought to 'make sense' of Buber's work with nature is that of unity. There is, it is alleged, a fundamental 'oneness' (identity, *unio mystica*) that all things and beings share and have in common *qua* being, and whatever relationality there be follows upon that 'oneness.' Yet the thing which some have focused on to account for the relation of which Buber speaks, is precisely that which makes this kind of relation impossible. Without the other's particularity being maintained in a radical way I cannot step into relation with this other and by virtue of that relation find myself having to do essentially with one who is thou to me. There are several variations of the unity model by means of which some have sought to reduce the seeming implausibility of standing in relation with the tree. The most venerable of these is the Thomistic solution. Although what to do with the tree is not the central problematic of his examination of Buber's view of God as person, Pedro Sevilla advances the relevance of the scholastic perspective as a way of dealing with the range of nature-human issues, while at the same time recognizing that this language of unity is far from what Buber himself had in mind.[81] Working from such a point of view one could, presumably, provide a metaphysical structure that accommodates both the oneness and the differentiation. Relation with the tree is possible, not because of the dryad 'in' the tree, but because the tree and I and everything else in creation partcipate in being; but I should not expect to find, nor be troubled by the absence of, any way for the tree to turn toward me since it is reason in its unity with my physical body which makes me of a different order of being from the tree, Anton Pegis makes this observation and seeks to move it as far as possible in an ecological direction.

No theology can speak of man or to man today unless it touches him in his unity with that world of nature which is more a part of his history and therefore a part of his own being, and which is reflecting more and more of his own spiritual engagement within it. Surely, we are in search of a theology of man in which his spiritual union with matter, beginning with the matter of his own body and extending across the earth toward outer space, is the central and paramount reality.[82]

But while such a notion of the unity of man and nature might give one some confidence in talking about the tree, it is of little usefulness in talking about the human person who considers the tree. The Thomistic envisagement builds on reason as the distinguishing human capacity, but Buber has tried to make it very clear that it is not reason as such which constitutes the capacity for relation, but human twofoldness which men and women share with no other things and beings, but by means of which the world is constituted for us in a twofold way. Yet the Thomistic way of thinking may itself yield a possible solution. That is the way of analogy. One of its most successful modern practitioners, E. L. Mascall, finds in the analogical character of the several acts of existing a way of seeing that could help:

> Even the lifeless ''it'' is the subject of an activity which enables it to be the object, and to contribute to, our own experience. In existing, it is not just passive, but is performing, on its own level of being, an activity—the activity of existing—which, on a vastly higher level and in the analogical mode proper to rational beings composed of soul and body, we too perform. If the radically analogical character of the act of existing is fully understood, we shall be able without falling into the fallacy of personifying the lower creation to recognize sub-human creatures, whether animals or inanimate, as partners with us in the hierarchical order of the universe to praise and glorify God.[83]

But this way of putting it is not free from the very danger which Mascall seeks to avoid; he thinks the way of analogy obviates the need to personify the subhuman, but himself speaks of the connection between the human and subhuman as a ''partnership,'' a term not unrelated to the danger of the pathetic fallacy. The more serious problem, however, is the disappearance of the essential humanity of human beings. Buber understands that:

> In Aquinas's world-system man is indeed a separate species of a quite special kind, because in him the human soul, the lowest of the spirits,

is substantially united with the human body, the highest of physical things, so that man appears as it were as 'the horizon and the dividing line of spiritual and physical nature.'[84]

But what is missing is the human wonder at "that in man which cannot be understood as a part of the world, as a thing among things."[85] There is no impulse to questioning self-confrontation. There is no wonder of man at himself.

A second variation of the unity model is provided by the wide range of philosophies which interpret the acknowledged continuities of human beings and nature by means of the root metaphor of evolution, process, becoming, development. The evolutionary teleology of Teilhard de Chardin is a case in point, particularly his pervasive sense of sacramentality which some have seen as having at least a formal resemblance to the sacramentality of Buber's world.[86] In Teilhard's view there is a single, unambiguous intentionality informing the movement from the pre-biotic cosmos to humanity in its present form and ultimately to the hyper-personal future of the universe. This purposiveness is the "sacramental presence of Christ as a radiating and energizing personal force which will ultimately permeate the whole creation."[87] Thus, instead of grace completing nature, as in the Thomistic convention, grace is built into the evolutionary process from the very beginning. As a corollary to this dynamic Teilhard rejects any substantial distinction between animate and inanimate matter. Even the most elemental aspect of creation has an incipient "within," not an impulse toward relationality, but at least a quality which anticipates responsiveness. To link the contention that every entity has such "an elementary beginning of perception and anticipation in extremely attenuated versions"[88] to the irreversibly hyper-personalizing movement of creation might seem to be advancing a different way of talking about Buber's distinction between the subthreshold, prethreshold, and threshold dimensions of subhuman nature. Teilhard's "Mass on the World" and the remarkable "Hymn to Matter" ("I bless you matter, and you I acclaim . . .")[89] apparently substantiate this connection. On this basis Teilhard was able, for example, to distinguish between the Hindu and Buddhist ways of being religious, on the one hand, with their presumption that "matter is dead weight and illusion," from the Christian way of being religious, on the other hand, with its presumption that "matter is heavily loaded, throughout, with sublime potentialities."[90] Yet the Christic character of the life which all entities share to some degree places an impossible burden on Buber's sense of things, if it is thought simply to offer a more comprehensive conceptual system for the same vision. It is not the entity in itself that has power, says Buber; and to speak of it sacramentally cannot involve one necessarily in an ineluctable Christian profession. Teilhard's metaphysics does not rephrase Buber's vision; it sees something altogether different.

Another variation of the unity model is appealed to in the special psychological orientation of Daniel Breslauer's *Guide to the Jewishness of Buber's "I and Thou"*.[91] For Breslauer the central problem of humanity is "dividedness," understood in a neo-Freudian way. The response to which Buber's work points, according to Breslauer, is a unification of the self, based on an affirmation of the self and world which simply declares their basic unity and wholeness. Prethreshold encounters, preserved by the ritual structure of *halacha,* enable the self to be united to the nonself.

> *I and Thou* opens with an invitation to perceive man's inevitable conflict, the divided existence which inexorably characterizes his life. Men inescapably live two different forms of existence. Each mode invariably gives way to the other, leaving men dual in their existence. At times we *experience* reality; the world appears as an object to be manipulated. External things are analyzed, defined, set at a distance and utilized as alien, non-self, and other. The self stands over against the non-self, defines its nature in contrast with others. Existence is a battle, a competition, a facing away from all that is not the self. At times, however, men enter into *relationship* and respond to the other (both human and nonhuman) as a partner in living. At such times reality is perceived as a unity of existence in which the self and non-self participate in a broader realm of being. Intimations of wholeness and

organic oneness are the residue from these encounters, these relationships.[92]

But Breslauer errs in identifying this twofoldness as "divided being" and as "man's melancholy fate."[93] The problem, as Buber sees it, is not our twofoldness, but the imperial pretensions of the objectifying attitude. The human lot is a melancholy one, not because we are divided from other things and beings, but because of the impossibility of securing continuity and permanence for the I-Thou relationships. As we have seen, this melancholy is not unrelieved. It is, in fact, exalted, as every I-Thou which has faded into the realm of I-It may return again and again to the realm of relation. So to seek a salvation by unification rather than in convenant[94] is to perceive both the human problem and its resolution in a way fundamentally different from Buber's version.

It seems, therefore, that all efforts to understand Buber's work with nature on the basis of a model of unity or unification cannot yield a satisfactory account of the matter. Neither the scholastic, the evolutionary, nor the psychological approach adequately safeguards or explains the possibility and the surprise of relation. I am concerned to show how a more satisfactory approach can be taken if one follows out certain conceptual suggestions internal to Buber, and regards with utmost seriousness Buber's own claim, in his response to Professor Levinas, ". . . that the relation of two beings to each other . . . does not in any sense mean their unification."[95] That Buber's assertion of a reciprocal relation with nature is "the most misunderstood and most often criticized part" of his philosophy[96] is not, after all, surprising. Buber's way of putting the matter is not always clear, and sometimes seems to invite the reader to pursue a hermeneutical line that is unnecessarily confusing. I do not see myself as playing the part of Buber's ontological butler, tidying up loose ends and cleaning up the debris after the master has entertained in the parlor. I do hope to show, however, that Buber's affirmation about nature can be so stated as to be a believable and integral aspect of his philosophy of relation.

Buber's schematic explanation in the Postscript to the second edition of *I and Thou* and his more modest explanatory comments scattered here and there in his works rest upon two basic contentions: first, the capacity to enter into meeting with other existing things and beings is native to humankind and to humankind alone;[97] second, there are "several different grades" of this capacity for mutuality,"[98] that is, there are degrees of mutuality. This view of mutuality is troublesome if and only if "degrees" is not understood metaphorically. Reciprocity might very well mean something quite different when one of the "partners" is nonhuman, but we should not understand this difference primarily in quantitative terms. Since Buber regularly speaks of mutuality as one of the essential ingredients in the I-Thou relation, his readers were led to wonder just what mutuality could really mean with the nonhuman, since what we ordinarily mean by "mutuality" would seem to be fundamentally excluded from such encounters. Buber himself recognizes that he always had to talk about the reciprocity of relation "with great reservations and qualifications."[99] Yet he also knew what had happened to him and to others. He knew that the fully human life involves us in an essential having to do with an other, and he believed himself to have been in an essential relation with the horse, the tree, etc. The task was to find an appropriate conceptual structure with which to speak intelligibly of the reality of his encounter. His choice of "mutuality" as the key quality of relation when it occurs in the interhuman sphere led him to talk about what met him in his natural encounters in terms of "mutuality" as well—i.e., the language of threshold, and gradations or degrees of mutuality. He wanted to be faithful to the actuality of the encounter while at the same time acknowledging the difference that being nonhuman makes. The resulting confusion led Diamond, among others, to observe that it would have been better "if Buber had given up the notion that [mutuality] is as applicable to a general description of the I-Thou encounter as are his other categories."[100]

What other schemes are open to us? One approach worries about a special status for the natural entities by virtue of which their dialogic power can be accounted for. Various theories of being are advanced, including variations of a doctrine of creation. This approach, as we have seen, seems always to develop a notion of what the human mode of being shares with other or all modes of being. That move grounds the dialogue but does not preserve the full ontological dimension of the other. It ends by appealing to a model which Buber explicitly rejects in most of its variations—pantheism ("a speculative oversimplification"), mystical union ("a mistaken interpretation"),[101] immersion/absorption ("a gigantic delusion).[102] I suggest we develop an approach which understands "*degrees* of mutuality" less quantitatively and more centrally as "modes (or kinds) of mutuality." This should allow us to concentrate on the relational attitude, informed by the paradigm of the inter-human, but focusing on it as an attitude, a way of regarding the totality of things and beings in the world, not a way of naming what thing or being, or aspect thereof, it is that is our partner, so to speak. Staying with relationality as an attitude, a way of perceiving the world, should help us avoid the conceptual turmoil and reduce the imprecision of other approaches. As a way of regarding all that meets us and that we meet, the attitude of relating turns us from an occupation with the I-Thou relation as a state, and frees us to be with the subhuman without speaking of it as if it were the protohuman. As attitude, relation frees us from speculating about it-beings and thou-beings, about persons and things, about means and ends. ". . . the essential is there, a person and what he stands over-against, which in this hour is, to begin with, only presence, not yet object, the contact of the unique with the unique, still prior to all transposition into the general."[103] Relation is simply a new way of looking at, of regarding the world which allows the land "not to be subjected to the will of man, but left to its own nature,"[104] a way of affirming the tree "as existing just as it is, in its own right, independently of our purposes."[105] The insight we can gain, however, from regarding relation as fundamentally attitudinal must not detract us from recognizing relation both as a "way of looking" and also a "way of affirming." Only in this manner will we be able to ground and safeguard conceptually the real, if not full, mutuality that comes from the impact of the unique otherness of the tree, the cat, the horse, the dog, the piece of mica upon us. This makes possible that essential quality of relation to which Maurice Friedman points in his perceptive and felicitous phrase, "the confirmation of otherness."

Of all the ways in which Buber speaks of relation, it is only *Gegenseitigkeit,* "mutuality," that presents a serious problem when applied "quantitatively" to the nonhuman spheres. His readers need to be conscious of the dangers involved in forgetting the nonliteral function of "degrees," and of the need to think in tems of "modes" of mutuality. His clarion is "Relation is mutuality."[106] "Relation is reciprocity."[107] But applied literally to the nonhuman, such a locution will alway be confusing. For what Buber wants and needs to say is that it is in our relating attitude to other things and beings that we become persons, not that the other thing or being becomes a person, unless he or she is human. There is no need to personalize the nonhuman things and beings of the world in relation to which we find our own life as persons occasioned. We become persons; the tree, the dog, the cat, or the horse do not. To speak of "mutuality" here can be at best only an oblique way of referring to the personalizing that happens to us in the encounter.

Something indeed happens, so to speak, to the other, whatever it may be; but the other does not in our relating attitude become a "person" thereby. This becomes clearer when we see that it is as attitude that the "idea" of relation gains scope and fertility beyond the interhuman sphere, even if some imprecision remains. (Dialogic theory as a whole seems destined to be characterized by some lack of precision, since the mystery of the other and of our finding ourselves standing in relation to the other is never reducible.) Buber himself saw this:

> I am concerned that the I-Thou relation be realized where it can be realized, and I cannot declare where it cannot be realized. I am concerned that the life of man be determined and formed by it. For I believe that it can transform the human world, not into something

perfect, but perhaps into something very much more human, according to the created meaning of man, than exists today. 108

We begin, then, as always with the depths of the interhuman sphere. Meeting there sheds light on or informs what is possible with the other spheres. To "consider a tree" after one has been in relation with another human being is to admit it to the sphere of nature where its independent being and space is, in that moment and from that perspective, allowed to be. The "philosophy of the relating attitude" does not require us to abandon our instrumental dealing with nature anymore than it requires us to abandon the scientific effort of knowledge and control. It requires of us only that we do not allow the objectifying attitude to exhaust what we have to do with the natural; that we use the natural in a caring way. The I-Thou attitude toward nature is a charter for the human care of the earth. The model is Kant's. Our treatment of the humanity in ourselves and in others, as an end in itself, does not preclude our treating it as a means; that treatment, however, does demand that our use of human beings must be consistent with their being ends in themselves. So it is with Buber. Our standing in relation to the natural does not preclude our using the natural as a means for the satisfaction of our needs; that using, however, must be consistent with allowing the natural now and again to be what it is apart from our purposes for it. In the grace of this attitude we are thus able to grant the natural appropriate freedom to be and to enter into relation with us, without the confusion of quantitative language. One might even want to say that it is only in such an attitude of grace and gratitude, born by our having come to be a person in relation to one another, that we are able really to allow the natural to be. In his memorable preface to the French edition of *I and Thou*, Gaston Bachelard anticipated this claim. "Of what importance to me," he wrote, "are flowers, trees, fire, and stone if I am without love and without a hearth? One must have been 'two' in order to understand the blue sky, in order to name a dawn. Infinite things like the sky, the forest and light only find their name in a loving heart." 109 An older, less poetic generation might have spoken of stewardship. Now it is our very care for the planet that is at stake. Indeed, as Samuel Rodin has argued,[110] the root crisis of our time is the "fragmentary atomistic world view of modern technological society" which manifests itself in a perspective toward the natural invironment which sees it as

> ...composed of an aggregate of separate resources, to be exploited by different groups of people, and each individual is fragmented into an aggregate of roles, diverse thoughts, motives, emotions, desires, goals, fears, personality traits, etc.[111]

Humanity, then, turns to control and manipulate the natural world of rocks, plants, and animals from which it has become estranged. This possessive form of life regards the environment in objectifying terms alone, subjecting it and organizing it as if it were a hostile force that needed to be subdued for human survival. The consequent destructiveness cannot be turned around without such a fundamental shift in attitude as Buber describes. Instead of seeing the human person as self-subsisting by virtue of his ability to control, we are invited to see the human person as coming to self-identity only in relation to all the things and beings with which one has to do, and whose otherness persists in each caring encounter. An attitude, then, of being at home in the world, of living as "friends of the earth," may enable us to regard the environment no longer as a thing to be managed, but as the many beings in relation to which we have discovered responsible life. As Martin Buber responded to Professor Hocking, "The experience from which I have proceeded and ever again proceed is simply this, that one meets another."[112] "If I face a human being as my Thou, and say the primary word I-Thou to him . . . he is Thou and fills the heavens. . . . All else," even the tree, "lives in his light."[113]

II. The Helper

Every I-Thou relationship, within a relation which is specified as a purposive working of one part upon the other, persists in virtue of a mutuality which is forbidden to be full.

—Martin Buber, *I and Thou*

*F*undamental to an appreciation of Buber's thought is the recognition that the mutuality of which he speaks admits of degrees. In Chapter One we saw how this contention helps us to understand the possibility of standing in an I-Thou relation with the tree when "degrees" is understood metaphorically, as "modes" rather than quantitatively. The mutuality of the I-Thou relation between a person and a tree is thus not so much "less than" that which is possible between two persons, but is a mutuality that is fitting, or appropriate to the situation. This judgment of appropriateness rather than a measure of quantity is also the key for understanding Buber's use of the term "fulness" with respect to the relational possibilities between two persons.

Mutuality arises in the sphere of the interhuman on two levels. The first is that level on which we have to do with another person without any defining task or role to be played out or performed, where mutuality is most fully possible. The second is that level on which we have to do with another person, where mutuality is genuinely possible but where we are prevented from becoming fully mutual. Since the Postscript to the 1957 edition of *I and Thou,* Buber spoke of this problem as the "normative limitation" on the fulness of mutuality which is occasioned by the presence of a task or a special defining role that is necessarliy involved.

There are situations of encounter between two persons which partake of the nature of mutuality but from which fulness is excluded, since there is a one-sidedness present. This one-sidedness makes it impossible for both partners to practice what Buber calls "inclusion," experiencing the relation from the other side, that is, from the point of view of the life situation of the other person. Buber's examples in this Postscript are the teaching, healing, and forgiving relations. An inequality is present in each, since in the nature of the case the pupil, the patient, the penitent cannot experience or view or know the relation from both sides; cannot, Buber says, practice inclusion. In this chapter I want to examine the concept of normative limitation (and its corollary, the practice of inclusion) as it arises in the sphere of the interhuman, between teacher and student (the learning relation), between physician and patient (the healing relation) and between priest and penitent (the forgiving relation).

After identifying the movements essential to mutuality, I shall try to account for Buber's rejection of the possibility of full mutuality (and thus the practice of inclusion) in each of these situations. Second, I shall explore the wider applicability of this principle. Third, I shall identify two problematic features of this paradigm of the helping relations, and will, finally, assess its significance in illuminating the dynamic of such task-defined relationships.

As we have seen, the most fundamental characteristic of our life as individual human beings is the "innateness of the longing for relation,"[1] the "impulse toward the other"[2] which Buber named, with metaphoric license, "the inborn Thou."[3] In the sphere of the human, "our life with men." there is no person, no situation, contact, or involvement with another human being that is excluded from the possibility of being a partner in dialogue—from the most fleeting and occasional, to the most stable and enduring. All discussion of degrees and the limitations on full mutuality must begin with this recognition of the universal human possibility of relation. Indeed, the latter would seem realistically to require the former. At the same time, fulness of mutuality is not inherent in our life together. "It is a grace, for which one must always be ready and which one never gains as an assured possession."[4]

Two movements are required for mutuality: distancing and

entering into relation. Modification of either movement will qualify the degree of fulness which is possible in a given relationship.

> By "meeting" in the pregnant sense in which I used the word, I understand an occurrence of the genuine I-Thou relation in which the one partner affirms and confirms the other as the unique person.[5]

This necessity to let the other be without being reduced or subsumed or absorbed is what Buber intends by "primal distancing" (*Urdistanzierung*), in which "I confirm and further my Thou in the right of his existence and the goal of his becoming, in all his otherness."[6] The importance of this setting at a distance cannot be over-emphasized, given the tendency of much superficial employment of Buber's thought to insist upon intimacy, closeness, harmony, and oneness as marks of authentic relation.

> ... once one ceases to regard the other as merely an object of observation and begins to regard the other as an independent other standing over against him, then we have the beginnings of the I-Thou relation.[7]

The second movement is entering into relation, an act whose fullest expression in the interhuman sphere includes mutual confirmation. In such an embracing or inclusion (*Umfassung*), one experiences the other side of the relationship, or more precisely, one experiences the relationship from the other side. One life opens up to another life, without one incorporating the other. This is "peculiarly characteristic of the human world."[8] As the overagainstness remains and necessarily so, there is, as Buber describes it, a "bold swinging into the life of the other." Other times he speaks of this as "imagining the real," that is "perceiving and thinking what is occurring in the mind and body of another individual."[9] Receiving such "an intimation of the being of the other,"[10] through inclusion or embracing is something like "empathy," although Buber himself explicitly rejects "empathy" as interchangeable with "inclusion" since he finds it too aesthetic a category, too open to an absorptionist perspective in which the otherness of the other is not sufficiently safeguarded. In his introduction to Buber's early work *Daniel*, in which the term "inclusion" (*Umfassung*) is used in this significant way, Maurice Friedman clarifies the movement of embracing in a helpful manner.

> "Experiencing the other side" means to feel an event from the side of the person one meets as well as from one's own side. It is an inclusiveness which realizes the other person in the actuality of his being, but it must not be identified with "empathy," which means transposing oneself into the dynamic structure of an object, hence, "the exclusion of one's own concreteness, the extinguishing of the actual situation of life, the absorption in pure aestheticism of the reality in which one participates." Inclusion is the opposite of this. "It is the extension of one's own concreteness, the fulfillment of the actual situation of life, the complete presence of the reality in which one participates." In inclusion one person, "without forfeiting anything of the felt reality of his activity, at the same time lives through the common event from the standpoint of the other."[11]

Along with the possibility of an I-Thou relation in the sphere of nature, the claim of the I-Thou relation to reciprocity or mutuality is a second feature of Buber's vision which has occasioned much misunderstanding and bewilderment. It seemed to the philosopher Levinas, among others, that the movement of real or primal distancing involves an asymmetry.[12] Buber's response should have been no surprise to anyone who had assimilated his claim that mutuality admits of degrees: "Mutuality in all it gradations cannot be regarded as the rule."[13] It is clearly a sensitive area, since Buber confessed that he always "had to talk about it [the reciprocity of the relation] with great reservations and qualifications."[14] The relation with God is not fully reciprocal, nor the relation with things and beings in the natural sphere. And it is not uncommon for someone to "stand over against another with less than complete presence and openness and yet not necessarily regard the other as It, as a mere object of observation and reflection . . ."[15] Hence, we are prepared for the more systematic application of the principle of gradation in the Postscript to particular instances in the sphere of the interhuman.

If Buber has indeed given us an insight into the distinctively human way of being in the world, then we should expect that every area of human thought and action would be illuminated when considered or participated in from the point of view of such a dialogic consciousness. Buber himself either developed or provided extensive clues for re-envisioning many of these areas—biblical hermeneutics, theater, political power, social theory, folk traditions. He also nominated the three examples of relationships between persons open thus to the possibility of mutuality but from which fulness of mutuality is normatively excluded. He wrote and lectured extensively on both the educative and therapeutic relationships, but of the pastoral relationship said little more than the single sentence in the Postscript to *I and Thou*.

I am concerned here to identify what Buber finds in each of these three relationships to constitute this normative limitation, without tracing the elaborate development of Buber's pedagogic and therapeutic theories. (1) The simplest and clearest statement of the pedagogical dilemma in *I and Thou* becomes the basis for the subsequent expansion of Buber's point of view in his lectures and addresses on education.[16]

> . . . the special educative relation could not persist if the pupil for his part practiced "inclusion," that is, if he lived the teacher's part in the situation.[17]

Everything quite obviously hangs on what Buber means by "the teacher's part." In a truly reciprocal conversation both sides are full and equal, but in the educative "conversation," as Buber sees it, one "has found direction" and the other "is finding it."[18] "The good teacher knows the soul of his pupils; the pupils would cease to be pupils if they knew the soul of their teacher."[19] The teacher trusts that the pupil "will become what he will become," while the pupil trusts that the teacher "is what he is."[20] These and other similar affirmations appear simply to be restatements of the inability of the pupil to experience the educative relationship from the side of the teacher; that is to say, nothing has yet been advanced to give any specific or empirical content to the differentiated "teacher's part." Little that is concrete appears until we move to Buber's description of what sort of thing it is that the educator does. That activity is essentially a curricular task. The teacher's task is to choose and to present to the pupil an effective world, to select "that in the world which will bring his students forth."[21] But this is to be done in such a manner as to respect the student's integrity.

In his anthologized and widely discussed article, "Freedom with Authority: A Buber Model for Teaching," John Scudder interprets such an approach to call for a "sharing of deep convictions between persons in a manner which respected and encouraged individuality," although the student "lacks the background and capacity to enter into the teacher's life in the same way that a teacher can imaginatively enter into the life of the student."[22] F. H. Hilliard correctly sees that for Buber the relationship is central in such a way as to avoid centering on the teacher (old style authoritarianism) or on the child (new style emphasis on freedom, creativity, and development).[23] He perceives Buber proposing a kind of synthesis of the best features of both, although Buber himself never used that or any other term that might appear in any way to compromise the concrete actuality and otherness of each of the partners in dialogue. Edward Kiner understands the teacher's part in such a situation to derive its authority not from knowledge or information about the world, but from "his ability to relate meaningfully with his students . . ."[24] Such an attitude, however, comes perilously close to the danger which Eugene Borowitz early recognized, namely, that learning might be displaced by relationship. To be sure, someone teaching as Buber suggests will consciously seek to avoid imposing his or her views on the pupil. Indeed, so strong was Buber's hostility against such interference and arbitrariness that he identified the real struggle of the modern world as not being". . . between East and West, or capitalism and communism, but between education and propaganda."[25] All of these suggestions, however, ignore the curricular core of the educator's task, the selection and presentation of an effective world to the student. The implication of this is that the relationship of both the teacher and the student to the text necessarily delivers the situation from being such that the relationship must be the sole bearer of meaning. This opens the way to the legitimate usefulness of discipline and structure, or in Borowitz's words, an openness to the sense "that role can be a means to humanhood," a continual reaching out to the student as a person.[26] The clarification of the text is what has brought teacher and student together. But since the teacher's indispensable part is the curricular one, in the broadest sense of the word, it is clear that, as Buber replied to the questions of Robert M. Hutchins, "an inclusive reciprocity between teacher and pupil neither should nor can exist."[27] But genuine, although limited, dialogue is possible. It is not clear, however, why friendhip between teacher and student is a barrier to the proper fulfillment of the educational enterprise, if the educator's part in that enterprise is essentially a curricular one.[28] Attitudinal and social problems, and the possible requirement of evaluative judgment might account for the necessary and normative limitation of the mutuality which may exist between teacher and pupil.

(2) The problematic of the therapeutic situation is analogous to that of the pedagogic situation and can be simply stated: depth healing occurs only in an I-Thou relation, with its noninstrumentality and its acceptance; but the mutuality of the relation is necessarily abridged by virtue of its asymmetrical requirement. The relationship is kept from moving into the fulness of mutuality by the very factors which have occasioned or brought it into being.

An elucidation of this problematic begins by recognizing that in Buber's model the genuine therapist "relates to his patients as a partner."[30] The dynamic of this partnership is trust; that is to say, a person becomes a patient by virtue of seeking assistance in dealing with a need from someone who can be counted upon to help. But as Jung observed,[31] it is a human being who comes seeking treatment, not a symptom or a syndrome. And healing becomes possible through the meeting[32] which avoids regarding the patient as an object of investigation and manipulation, or which sees that patient simply as an illustration of some conceptual psychological model, such as the Oedipus complex, inferiority feeling, collective archetype. The therapist's function is to aid in the regeneration of the patient's "atrophied personal centre."[33] This is possible only in the person-to-person encounter, that is, in the mutuality of the I-Thou; but it cannot happen unless the therapist experiences the effect of his own action. That is, the therapist does and must do something "that the patient cannot do."[34] And so, that which makes therapy "work" is precisley that which imposes a normative limitation on the mutuality possible.

Two other ways of estimating the source of this normative limitation in the therapeutic situation have been proposed by interpreters who are sympathetic to Buber's vision and who seek to develop views of the healing process that are consonant with his. A brief reference to both of them may help to clarify Buber's view, which, in the end, is really quite different.

Gutsch and Rosenblatt, for example, derive the asymmetrical character of the healing relation from the nature of the patient's problem rather than from the nature of the therapeutic or counseling task.

> Many ... clients are so emotionally disturbed that they find it difficult to reciprocate in dialogue simply because they cannot bring themselves to make decisions nor to openly express their opinions about the decision they would like to make.[35]

In their influential article they identify other popular ways of accounting for what they call "dialogue blockage": nonproductivity (Fromm), self-alienation (Horney), other-directedness (Riesman), psychoneurosis (Freud).[36] But these are all variant descriptions of the sickness. For Buber, however, the limitation on mutuality does not derive from analysis of the disease, but from what is analytic of the situation itself, the impossibility of the patient experiencing the relation from the side of the therapist. That is impossible in the nature of the case.

A different picture of the impossibility is given in Adolf Guggenbühl-Craig's insightful work *Power in the Helping Professions*.[37] A fully reciprocal relationship may be lived out sexually, but a therapeutic relationship must not be. The irrevocable "no" spoken to the living out of sexuality in analysis is not required by any legal or moral standard, conventionally understood, so far as he can see. The "iron rule of analysis that sexuality between analyst and patient must under no circumstances be lived out"[38] is based on his conviction that the object of therapy is healing, that is, the achievement of a new psychic orientation in the patient, no matter how mutual the psychic influence of patient and analyst is. The object of therapy is not the relationship between the analyst and patient; were the sexuality between them to be lived out, the relationship would, in his view, be transformed into an end in itself, thus making healing impossible.

It does not follow, however, that a mutual sexual attraction between physician and patient, in itself, that is, the awakening of sexual fantasies, is to be rejected in the same way. Buber himself understood the educative (and by analogy, the therapeutic) relation to be "completely unerotic."[39] That this excluding necessarily follows from Buber's own standpoint is not altogether clear, as we shall explore later. Guggenbühl-Craig seems to insist that everything depends on "what this sexuality really expresses,"[40] since the wholeness of the persons present to one another here really includes the physical, hence erotic, dimension. Even in a relation with the limited mutuality of the psychotherapeutic one, "true eros does not involve wanting to impose our own plan, or our own ideas, on others."[41] Hence, such sexual fantasies might indeed have a positive effect on the therapy.[42]

As much as Gutsch and Rosenblatt and Guggenbühl-Craig

intend fidelity to Buber's originary therapeutic insight, and agree on the asymmetrical character of the relationship between physician and patient, they both locate the source of the asymmetry elsewhere—one, in the nature of the problem that moves a person to become a patient; the other, in the threat of lived out sexuality to focus attention on the relationship itself, thus transforming it into an end in itself.

(3) The problematic of the sacerdotal relationship is the most obvious of the three special examples to Buber, although it is the one about which both he and his commentators have had the least to say.

> The most emphatic example of normative limitation of mutuality could be provided by the pastor with a cure of souls, for, in this instance an "inclusion" coming from the other side would attack the sacral authenticity of the commission.[43]

At the outset it should be observed that it is not at all clear just how this relationship should be designated. In the Postscript (according to Smith's translation) Buber speaks of the pastor and his cure. In "Healing through Meeting" he speaks about the priest as one who is "armed with sacred possessions of divine grace and holy word."[44] If we keep in mind the obvious implication of this being a third example of an I-Thou relation from which full mutuality is excluded, then we should expect Buber to be talking about the priest's or the pastor's side in this relationship as one which by definition or in the nature of the case could not be entered into fully by the person on the other side. The term "pastor" points, however, more to a functional rather than an essential difference; hence, "pastoral" may be too weak a way to designate this third type. It is not without interest that in his translation of the Postscript ("Afterword"), Kaufmann, who was deeply offended by attempts to Christianize Buber's invitation, "rabbinized" this passage so as to make "pastoral" a more appropriate designation than the text can bear. The limitation, according to Kaufmann, concerns not priests or even pastors, but "those charged with the spiritual well-being of their congregation."[45] Kaufmann may have been led to paraphrase here in order to make the example fit the contemporary understanding of the relation of a rabbi ("spiritual leader") to his congregation, but in so doing he has misperceived the nature of what is at stake in this third example of the normative limitation of mutuality.

On the basis of the few direct remarks we have from Buber, it seems that the best designation for this third example of limitation would be something like "sacerdotal," some term which focused on the peculiar capacity arrogated to or claimed by/for the Christian priesthood (Roman, Orthodox, Anglican, Old Catholic, non-Chalcedonian) to grant or to pronounce absolution from confessed sin. Hence we speak of "forgiving" in a sacerdotal relationship, paralleling "healing" in a therapeutic and "learning" in an educative relationship. This seems clearly in accord with the sacramental/priestly/sacredotal emphasis with which Kurzweil perceives Buber's comments about the "pastor."

> ... mutual inclusion would in this case completely disable him from fulfilling the sacramental commission of the priest and would, especially in the case of the Roman Catholic priest, undermine his status as a Father-Confessor.[46]

Such an interpretation fits with Buber's elucidation of the spheres in which one has to do with guilt: legal and social guilt, for which reconciliation is to be made; and guilt in relation to faith, for which confession, repentance, and penance are in order.[47] Kaufmann's translation ("spiritual well-being of their congregation") is more open to understanding the relation in plural rather than single categories, a misunderstanding of the I-Thou relation avoided by Friedman's insistence on the singularity of the person and the unrepeatability of the guilt.[48]

That which the priest is believed in the traditions of catholic Christianity to be able to do, and is granted power and permission by virtue of ordination by bishops in the apostolic succession to do, is to consecrate, to bless, and to absolve, and that on the basis of the "sacred possessions of divine grace." The forgiveness which a penitent is able to give to himself or to herself is not of the same order as that which the priest, by virute of being a priest, is understood to be able to give. Hence, the priest-penitent relation is by definition asymmertical.

We are now in a position to see more clearly the grounds for Buber's rejection of the possibility of full mutuality (and thus the practice of inclusion from both sides) in some situations:

> Every I-Thou relationship, within a relation which is specified as a purposive working of one part upon the other, persists in virtue of a mutuality which is forbidden to be full.[49]

Each of these situations, the necessary if not sufficient condition of which is the performance of a task, has by virtue of the personal encounter of the two human beings the possibility and requirement of dialogic life, but also, by virtue of the asymmetrical nature of the task, a restriction of fulness, with respect to mutuality or reciprocity. Genuine learning, healing, and forgiving occur only in the noninstrumentality and acceptance of the I-Thou relation. But the pupil, the patient, and the penitent each has a need, arrangements for the meeting of which introduce elements which qualify not only mutuality but also each of the other basic characteristics of relation.

(a) I-Thou is exclusive, that is, one relates to the other in wholeness of being; one does not attend to the other in such a way as to select out objective characteristics, to focus on particular aspects of the other. The three situations under consideration are exceptions because the wholeness is abridged. It is the teacher's knowledge, the physician's skill, the priest's sacramental power which, in each case, forms the basis on which they are sought out by the ignorant, the sick, and the guilty. And it is the other's ignorance, sickness, or guilt that is to be "treated." Indeed, the appropriateness of just such transitive verbs suggest how nonreciprocal these relations must be.

(b) I-Thou is brought into being in a twofold way: through grace and by an act of will: "The Thou meets me" and "I step into direct relation" with the other.[50] But there is no deliberation here, no estimation, no sorting or seeking out, only a turning toward the other who has turned toward me. The three situations under consideration are exceptions because this turning toward the other is made conditional and selective.

(c) I-Thou is immediate, lived in the present, without temporal awareness or reckoning. No conceptual scheme, no apparatus of desire or planning, no categories of interpretation are used. The three situations under consideration are exceptions because each is permeated by a consideration of means.

(d) I-Thou is mutual, with each partner in the relation affecting the other. The three situations under consideration are exceptions because both partners may not, in principle, practice inclusion equally. One seeks what the other has to give; the other waits to give until he or she is sought out.

Wholeness, grace, immediacy, and mutuality, then, are all qualified in each of the three situations by virtue of one or another aspect of the task or function which defines the relationship. Without the implementation of the task, there would be no necessary barrier to full relation.

We have seen that the defining presence of an agreed upon task in a relationship between two persons makes the equal practice of inclusion impossible, thus normatively limiting the mutuality of that relationship. Buber's illustrations of such situations have been from three professions (teacher, physician, clergy, to which he once also added a fourth, a lawyer[51]), in each of which there is acknowledged or claimed an expertise or power which cannot be shared or experienced by the one needing the service without the relation being transformed into something else. In the next section I shall examine some of the problematic features of such a professional paradigm. I want first and here to speculate on the possibility of its wider applicability, beyond the range of nonsharable tasks with their assumption of unique skill or knowledge.

We cannot understand Buber on this point without recognizing that the two primary words, the two world-defining attitudes, are not, in themselves, descriptive of all experiences and all relations. They are definitive of what it means to "experience" and to be in "relation" with. There are many gradations in the realm of I-It, determined by the ever increasing distance from relation. There are also many gradations in the realm of I-Thou, determined by the ever increasing distance from experience and use. The professional situations are a specific case of relation still continuing certain aspects of use by virtue of the task. There is every reason to think that there are many other situations from which full mutuality is excluded to a similar if different degree, yet in which there is sufficient distance from simple use as to constitute them as instances of I-Thou relation. Buber himself speaks about the glimmer of such a relationship even in fleeting and momentary encounters. Hence, we can add such other partnerships as might occur in social work, supervisory and managerial or administrative connections, commercial and service transactions, employer-employee relations, all situations that involve judgment, evaluation, and probation (all of which are elements of use) but in which trust and acceptance are present in the degree to have the situations perceived as being sufficiently distant from experience (I-It). All "helping" relationships are necessarily one-sided, in the same way as the professional situations discussed earlier, and that by virtue of the defining presence of a task, role, function, or purpose.[52]

Harvey Cox and Walter Kaufmann are among those commentators who are sensitive to the need for a wider applicability of the principle of limitation such as we have been suggesting here. They both assume, however (and mistakenly, I think) that such an extension goes beyond what Buber himself envisioned or beyond what a strict application of his categories would allow. In *The Secular City* Harvey Cox reflects on the problems and possibilities of humanizing life in an urban, technological setting. Human relationships, he is convinced, do "not have to be lifeless or heartless" in the city "just because they are impersonal."[53] According to Cox, we need to designate a third type of relationship, "I-You," between I-It and I-Thou which would

. . . include all those public relationships we so enjoy in the city but which we do not allow to develop into private ones. These contacts can be decidedly human even though they remain somewhat distant. . . . The danger with an I-Thou typology is that all relationships which are not deeply personal and significant tend to be swept or shoved into the I-It category. But they need not be. The development of an I-You theology would greatly clarify the human possibilities of urban life. . . . [It could describe] very well the rewarding relationship one has with a fellow team member, with whom one has worked on a research project or painted a house. It derives from work that is done together by two persons for whom the work is the key to their mutuality.[54]

Cox is surely consistent with Buber in maintaining that all public and private encounters between persons ought to be "decidedly human," that many of our public, urban meetings in which an element of use appears ought to be human, even if they are not "deeply personal and significant." Cox errs, however, in supposing that Buber's view and categories do not call for and allow precisely this humanizing move; he makes a more fundamental mistake, however, in supposing that Buber intends the two primary words or attitudes to be descriptive of all experience and relation in the sense that all relationships would be purely one or the other. As we have seen, the principle of gradation applies to both.

In his essay, "Dialogue," Buber responds to an opponent who makes an objection quite similar to Cox's. The situation is not "all or nothing," according to Buber.

Into nothing exalted, heroic or holy, into no Either and no Or, only into this tiny strictness and grace of every day, where I have to do with just the very same "reality" with whose duty and business I am taken up in such a way, glance to glance, look to look, word to word, that I experience it as reached to me and myself to it, it as spoken to me and myself to it.[55]

Buber's distinctive insight is that nothing lies outside the possibility of relation, of mutuality on some level, to some degree. The typology of the two standpoints functions not to prescribe the nature of all possible experience and relation, nor

to describe the empirical content of all experiences and relations; the typology serves simply to alert us to what enhance-
ment of our life might be possible as we turn toward the other.

Kaufmann's use of "I-You" in his translation has nothing
in common with Cox's concern for a human but not fully personal
type of relation. Precisely the opposite. Kaufmann has traded
"Thou" for "You" in part because he felt that "Thou" was too
destructive of the pervasive intimacy of Buber's book. I have
earlier noted that since the use of "You" confuses nominative
and objective cases, singular and plural forms, it is less useful
for what Buber wants to say. Yet the intimacy about which
Kaufman is concerned is surely as much a matter of degree as
that of mutuality. In his own way Kaufmann also insists on the
manifold modes or relation in which treating the other as a
means does not necessarily or completely move the relation all
the way to the realm of I-It.

> The total encounter in which You is spoken with one's whole being is
> but one mode of I-You. And it is misleading if we assimilate all the
> modes of I-You to I-It.[56]

Kaufmann's appeal to Kant in support of this interpretation is
appropriate and is one of the most helpful paragraphs in his
otherwise eccentric and peculiar "I and You— A Prologue."

> Kant told men always to treat humanity, in our person as well as that
> of others, as an end also and never only as a means. This is one way of
> setting off I-You from I-It. And when he is correctly quoted and the
> "also" and the "only" are not omitted, as they all too often are, one
> may well marvel at this moral wisdom.[57]

The two standpoints which Kant identifies as the ways in which
the human self could regard itself and interpret the self's
movements in the world are the clear philosophical antecedents
of the two basic attitudes in which one may, according to Buber,
stand with respect to the things and beings of the world. Kant's
two standpoints are not identical with Buber's two primary
words, of course, and Kant's interest, unlike Buber's, is more

epistemological than existential. The connection is as follows. We may regard the self as an agent, an initiator who acts on the presupposition of freedom. And we may regard the self as acted upon, as one whose movements are not, strictly speaking, acts at all, but instances of behavior which can be accounted for in the nexus of causal explanations. The similarity to Buber is extensive, even if it is not total. The I-It attitude is the charter for the scientific, causal understanding of human beings in the world: estimation, calculation, planning, testing, replication. The I-Thou attitude is the self understood as stepping in freedom into relation with the other. Buber's concern is to open up possibilities for the humanization of life; Kant's concern is, in the *Grundlegung* at least, to develop a standard for judging the putative moral worth of the maxims of certain acts, that is, he aims to establish the possibility of moral knowledge.

> Act in such a way that you always treat humanity whether in your own person or in the person of any other, never simply as a means, but always at the same time as an end.[58]

Kaufmann correctly identifies one aspect of the formulation in question which helps us to understand how a situation could be essentially I-Thou even with the presence of task, function, purpose, utility. It is analogous to treating the humanity in oneself or in any other person always as end but at the same time, although in a nonessential manner, as means. The other aspect of Kant's formulation with which he reveals his hand is the language form "treat humanity," that is to say, he uses a transitive construction, an objectifying verb precisely in the formulation in which he invokes the necessity of freedom, and without contradiction. The presence of means does not disqualify the maxim from having a claim to moral worth (Kant), nor remove the situation from the realm of I-Thou (Buber). The use of "also" and "only" ("simply" and "always" in the Paton translation used here) is thus essential to Kant's purpose, and is the linguistic precedent for the principle of gradation in Buber. In this way Kant helps us understand how a principle such as the normative limitation of mutuality in the helping situations can have general applicability.

(Kant's program cannot, of course, be taken uncritically as an anticipation of or early statement of Buber's point, since the "humanity" under consideration in Kant's formulation of the end-in-itself refers to our rational nature alone, and Buber speaks, rather, of our "whole being.")

━━━━━━━━━━━

The long-range usefulness of Buber's paradigm of relation-without-full-inclusion may be increased by considering two of its problematic features. (1) First, for each of the three situations under consideration the models which Buber consciously employs or to which he unconsciously appeals may very well be unnecessarliy restrictive. Each of these three situations can be conceptualized in a different way, and frequently is, so as to avoid the starkness of the subject-object-in-relation (already qualified by Buber's admission of them all to the humanizing potential of I-Thou mutuality), and, at the same time, to increase the degree of reciprocity that could be considered appropriate to the situation. Buber may have been led to the concept of single inclusion by virtue of the peculiarity of the models of these three situations with which he was working. Consistent with the intentionality of Buber's analysis, each of these situations could be envisaged as more rather than less reciprocal, and as less sharply distinguished from each other. This language about models might seem to be inappropriate, in principle, to Buber's philosophy of the interhuman, since the picture of mutuality has always been more characterized by trust than by a reliance on methods and techniques, such as the employment of models. There seems to be no way of gainsaying the fact that in the living out of relation the conscious use of models introduces a destructive, distancing and objectifying aspect. To employ a model is to relate to the other in terms of precedent categories, and involves the educator, the therapist, or the absolver in the danger of imposing himself or herself on the other as pupil, patient, or penitent. To employ models brings into awareness the other in terms of such factors as behavior, skill, and intellect, [59] rather than genuine encounter, and points up the problem of what has been called the "power shadow"; [60] that is, the problem of dealing with motiviation "to help" another, which can be an uncounscious assertion of oneself over the other.

A different sort of reason for rejecting the deliberate utilization of models is suggested by the imprecision that seems to attach to some of the conventional models for these situations. Many commentators on the wider usefulness of Buber's dialogic insights have noted how the lines distinguishing the action of one profession from the other so easily blur. Since one of the central "achievements" of an educator is to "create genuine human encounter," the educator becomes, as Borowitz observes, essentially a healer, especially in an anti-human time. [61] Craig has suggested the way in which the successful social worker is also to be thought of as a therapist, healing a diseased social situation. [62] Since some consider the pathology of a situation ordinarily described as a sickness to be primarily a problem of inadequate perception of the realm of the interhuman, Rioch believes that the ". . . whole process of psychotherapy would be much better understood if it were conceived as educational rather than curative." [63] The chief burden of most contemporary discussion of the forgiving relationship is concerned to locate it in a pastoral rather than a sacerdotal context, emphasizing psychological (that is, healing) rather than sacramental factors. The positive side of all of this blurring of professional lines is highlighted in Friedman's reference to what he calls the therapeutic possibilities of all dialogue. [64]

Another expression of this role imprecision does not so much involve the blurring of professional lines as the blurring of the distinction between the partners in each of the situations under consideration. This is not the same problem as the issue of normative limitation which is more a matter of role definition. The issue at hand concerns the empirical realities of human imperfection, fallibility, and weakness. The teacher, physician, and priest in any relation is not an abstract, or theoretical ideal type,

but a human being, with all the achievement, skill, awkward-
ness, and error that characterizes even the most competent
professional. Such a recognition of the "human" dimension
actually is quite consistent with the critical element of dialogue,
which as Frankenstein sees it, is "the inter-changeability of the
subject-object positions."[65] In all the situations defined by the
working out of a purpose, the helper also needs help, or at least
should be understood as potentially needing help. Living out a
purposive relationship in the light of that recognition can
empower the implementation of the defining task without the
rigid sense of hierarchy which is always the enemy of mutuality.
While the helper accepts the asymmetricality of the relationship, he or she can thus open the self to be affected by all the
impulses that proceed from the person of the pupil, the patient,
or the penitient.[66] That is possible because power over the other
does not belong essentially to this archetypal situation. The
central fact is for the healer to be able to affirm his or her own
woundedness. Psychologically this means, in the healing situation for example, "that the patient has a physician within
himself, but also that there is a patient in the doctor, neither side
of which should be repressed."[67] This should give the patient
and therapist a way of regarding with equal authority and equal
validity the way in which they see life. The therapist and the
patient could thus be on the same *plane,* so to speak,[68] without
compromising the one-sided nature of the skill/insight and need
that brought the two persons together initially.

  Wounded healers

> . . . are, so to speak, themselves constantly being analyzed and
> illuminated by their patients. Such an analyst recognizes time and
> again how the patient's difficulties constellate his own problems and
> vice versa, and he therefore openly works not only on the patient, but
> on himself. He remains forever a patient as well as a healer.[69]

The pedagogical analogue, of course, would make provision for
the teacher to be a learner throughout the educative moment, as
well as the pupil. Such a suggestion would perhaps require the
educative task to shifted away from being a curricular task at

its center, and be moved toward mutual nourishment in one another's presence, in which there are some ingredients of the sharing-of-life pattern after the fashion of the master-apprentice relationship.[70] The sacerdotal analogue is more difficult to suggest since the sacramental act of absolving appears, outside the context of faith in which it is properly set, to depend on a hermeneutics of magic. Since Vatican II the Christian world has, however, been moving toward recovering a more authentic notion of forgiveness in which the situation of the priest and penitent is not conceptualized in so individualistic a manner. Sin is acknowledged to be mutual, from both sides, and the absolution that is conveyed is not thought of simply as a substance dispensed from one toward the other, but a reconciliation and renewal which both minister to each other in the community of faith.

We need to think of these helping relationships in such a way as to regard the participants as being essentially on the same human plane, without eliminating all dimensions of one-sideness, and for the participants themselves so to regard each other. The presupposition for such a regarding is the mutual confirmation of one another's humanity. Such an act necessarily means a recognition and acceptance of the psychophysical unity of each of the partners, each attending to the other as a whole person, to what in another metaphysical climate would have been described as "body and soul," and what Friedman has called "the eros of dialogue."[71] This seems to be related to the sort of thing that Haim Gordon was aiming at in his proposal for a way of clarifying the content of I-Thou relationships.[72] He asks us to avoid defining and classifying these relationships and invites us instead to illustrate them personally.

The sensuous content needs to be present in all relational situations, although it must not be isolated or identified as such, that is, it must not be deliberately or consciously present, since this kind of move is objectifying and characteristic of the I-It attitude. Buber himself was not unaware of this need and its complication. Alas for the situation characterized by "mismeeting" when the wholeness of a personal identity is diminished.[73] Several people have written in a moving fashion of the warmth and unreserve of their personal encounters with Buber, or of those they have witnessed. Benjamin Wolman, for example, interpreted his perception of some American students in Israel as Buber lectured in this way:

> I couldn't help marveling at the rapidly growing bond between the Prophet and his disciples. Words were not everything; it was a magnetic force that pulled the young people to Buber . . . Buber never talked down to people; he conversed with them as equals . . . Only truly great men can preserve this child-like simplicity and immediacy in human relations.[74]

Aubrey Hodes remembers Buber's face "so alert and receptive, so rockfast and free, so open to the presence of his companion."[75] Because of this radical openness, Hodes conjectured that it is as "a great teacher, embracing consideration of the whole of human existence in his approach to his pupils that would occasion Buber's most enduring influence on our time."[76] As a teacher Buber was primarily concerned with "how to give the pupil a sense of his identity, of his organic unity; how to show him the way to responsibility and love."[77]

> Everything depends on the teacher as a man, as a person. He educates from himself, from his virtues and his faults, through personal example and according to circumstances and conditions. His task is to realize the truth in his personality and to convey this realization to the pupil.[78]

At the same time other commentators on Buber's educational philosophy and activities have noted that Buber himself seemed often to be way of the sensuous content of I-Thou relations,[79] generally shunning personal contact, that is, the friendly embrace, with others. Haim Gordon made a careful, largely unnoticed inquiry, to discover whether Buber ever realized in his own educational practice the significance of "developing open dialogical relations with each pupil."[80] His survey of the available data convinced him that "correctness and a lack of spontaneity characterized many of Buber's educational and personal relationships."[81] Gordon believes that the source of this reticence was the pedagogical climate of Hapsburg Austria and both Imperial and Weimar Germany in which Buber had lived and which Gordon is convinced guided him thoughout his life. This climate, according to Stephan Zweig, whose reconstruction Gordon takes as essentially correct,

> . . . suppressed desires and feelings, disregarded the human body as a source of joyful, physical expression and of knowledge, and repressed freedom and openness in human relations. Decorum and propriety was then an ultimate concern; the body was deemed to exist primarily in order to serve the intellect; openness meant intellectual openness and dialogue meant a meeting of the minds. . . .[82]

Such an interpretation seems largely conjectural, and one ought not to accept uncritically such an evaluation of Buber's teaching. Furthermore, even were one to find such ancedotal information about Buber's personal life to be interesting, and Zweig's assessment of European culture a plausible if unconscious model for Buber's pedagogical style, this type of inquiry has, in principle, little relevance to deciding the conceptual issue with respect to the manner in which participants in dialogue might be on the same plane, present wholly (that is, bodily as well, sensuously, erotically) to one another, yet without overcoming the one-sidedness which the task at hand creates. At best such an inquiry can only encourage us to be less wary that Buber was of the physical dimension in I-Thou relations, particularly in the three situations under consideration.

(2) A second problematic feature of Buber's paradigm of relation-without-full-inclusion concerns the alleged threat of structure to a life of relation. Structure (task, role, purpose, definition, the arrangement for bringing together teacher and pupil, therapist and patient, priest and penitent) has conventionally been regarded as the enemy of relation with its characteristic spontaneity and openness. I have suggested in the preceding analysis that in the three situations under consider-

ation the one-sidedness of the need (to know, to be healed, to be forgiven) does not necessarily have to be thought of in such absolute or so radical a fashion. Even if it were, it does not follow, even on Buber's grounds, that the relation is essentially deprived of full mutuality.

Structure provides the continuity necessary for the pre-servation and sustenance of human life. It stands in dialectical relationship to the objectifying attitude as both its possibility and product. It is an absolute necessity since we are not disem-bodied intellects or discarnate spirits; since, that is, there is an irreducible materiality to human existence. Absolute asceticism is not a human possibility. The elemental needs of life could not be satisfied apart from the careful guidance and employment of structure in all the variety of its modes. The choice, for example, cannot be between attending with reverence to the things and beings of the world, or to things and beings spiritual, to God, to the realm of the spirits, etc. The world will be attended to willy nilly, and that by means of structure. The choice can only be between ways of attending to that world of materiality; that is, the choice can only be between a concern with structure which makes for openness to relation and a concern with structure which closes off or reduces the possibility of relation. The other with whom one may stand in relation is a concrete, material thing or being, not an idea or essence. It is the wholeness of that thing or being with whom one is in relation, and that includes, in an undifferentiated way, materiality as manifested and known in and through structure. If by the I-It attitude we understand the utilization of structure, then we could para-phrase Buber's famous summary of the first part of *I and Thou* by observing that "without structure man cannot live. But he who lives with structure alone is not a man."[83]

A dialogic hermeneutic of constancy will disclose that structure itself is not the enemy of relation but only that attitude toward structure which regards it as guaranteeing and exhaust-ing the meaning or possibilities for life; not continuity in itself, but the thirst for continuity destroys relation..

In his foreword to Donald J. Moore's *Martin Buber, Prophet*

of Religious Secularism, Maurice Friedman sounds the caution
that so many readers and interpreters of Buber miss altogether.

> What Buber does say repeatedly is that structure is necessary as well as
> spontaneity—not just any structure, but *structure* that makes spon-
> taneity possible, planning that leaves room for surprises.—Here, as
> elsewhere in Buber's thought, it is not I-Thou *or* I-It which is the
> basic choice but the healthy alternation between I-Thou and I-It. It is
> this alternation that allows every It to be taken again into the meeting
> with the Thou, every structure to brought again and again into the
> meeting between person and person, community and community,
> people and God, mortal I and 'eternal thou.'[84]

If this analysis is a correct elucidation of Buber's fundamental insight, then we should not expect that the structure of
task or purpose in the three situations under consideration
should necessarily and in principle be a barrier to mutuality.
Indeed, in his own statement of the principle of normative
limitation, Buber gives a clue, consistent with the foregoing
interpretation, which makes less absolute the very limitation
under discussion. Notice how Buber puts it:

> Every I-Thou relationship, within a relation which is specified as a
> purposive working of one part upon the other, persists in virtue of a
> mutuality which is forbidden to be full.[85] (Smith translation)

> Every I-You relationship is a situation defined by the attempt of one
> partner to act on the other one so as to accomplish some goal depends
> on a mutuality that is condemned never to become complete.[86]
> (Kaufmann traslation)

Buber suggestively distinguishes between the helping
liaison itself ("relation" [Smith], "situation" [Kaufmann]), and
the mutuality ("relationship" [Smith and Kaufmann]) which is
possible in that helping liaison apparently to varying degrees.
What is going on in this suggestion can perhaps be made clear if
we designate the helping liaison as "relationship" and the
I-Thou mutuality which becomes possible in that liaison as
"relation." Accordingly, we can say that the pedagogic, thera-

peutic, and sacerdotal liaisons are relationships which are characterized by order, procedure, rite, and duration. As such we may describe these relationships as coming into being and persisting so long as the task or purpose defines the contact. Relation, on the other hand, is a possible aspect of such continuing purposive relationships. The one-sidedness of the helping relationship does not, in principle, have to extend in the same way to the relation itself. Indeed, the goal is to humanize the relationships in the I-Thou attitude, to permeate all relationships with relation. In this way structure can be a vehicle of mutuality, as it were, rather than its obstacle.[87]

We are in a position finally to indicate the way in which such a reconsideration of the problem of "normative limitation" illuminates the dynamic of the helping relationships. The relationships are defined by the assertion of need and the arrangement to respond to that need: structure. But the choice is not between structure and spontaneity, but between regarding structure as closure and as enabling, as an opening. Nor is the choice between the constancy of need (and its response) and the fleeting moments of mutuality. Buber himself provides the clue: "all else lives in its light."[88] In the light, that is to say, of one's having stood in relation. The world of things and beings, even of tasks, needs, and purposes, is not the same after one has been in relation. In order to emphasize the uncontrollability of relation, its nontransitive character, that the stepping into relation is a response to the grace of being met, the mutuality of the I-Thou relation is sometimes said to be momentary, a flash, an instant followed perhaps by another in some other time and place, but in no connected way. As a temporal metaphor this way of speaking points radically to the context of freedom, and this can neither be gainsaid nor discarded. What is possible and necessary to be emphasized now is the continuing significance, an alteration in perspective, happening to one as a consequence of standing in relation. After one has stood in relation, one can no longer live with, use, or 'deal with' the things and beings of the world in the same objectifying way.

This produces what Buber called the "only authentic assurance of continuity," [89] to be contrasted with the "thirst for continuity" that seeks spatial and temporal security by means of structural transformations. Our natural tendency is to transform relation into an experience than can be located, staked down, in space and time, since it is by such an approach that our knowledge about the world is secured. But the kind of continuity appropriate to relation is of another sort. From the point of view of one who has stood in relation, the world of It, the structure of need and its response, has a new, nonthreatening status. Such a person finds himself entering again and again into the world of It with a kind of expectancy, a kind of reverence which he did not have before for all the things and beings because one or another of them has been the vehicle or the occasion, the minister or partner of relation. The It-world is preserved in its own necessary distance and integrity, but that world has been transformed, has been penetrated by relation.

In connection with the three relationships or situations under consideration, it would appear that the goal consistent with and appropriate to Buber's fundamental concern would be something like the following. The teacher, therapist, and priest can enter into a relationship with a pupil, a patient, or a penitent without a prior determination of arbitrary limits and with an openness to the presence and increase of mutuality. Buber's invitation to the maximal humanizing of all our encounters is extended as well to these three situations. The relationships as such are task oriented and purpose defined. But within each one the partners may move into relation with its potential for mutuality and reciprocity, without any preliminary assessment of degrees. The normative limitation attaches to the relationship, not to the relation as such. And so the 'fulness' which attaches to encounters which are not task-defined does not differ from that which is possible in these three situations so much in a quantitative way. The difference is a qualitative matter, relevant to the nature of the encounter. The presence of a task to be performed does not seal the borders of mutuality. Being 'near' or 'far' from relation, being 'fully' or 'partially' mutual is not a distinction to be measured, but a recognition that each relationship is open to mutuality in it own peculiar way. [90]

III. The Brother

I firmly believe that the Jewish community in the course of its renaissance, will recognize Jesus; not merely as a great figure in its religious history, but also in the organic context of a Messianic development extending over millennia, whose final goal is the Redemption of the world. But I believe equally firmly that we will never recognize Jesus as the Messiah Come, for this would contradict the deepest meaning of our Messianic passion. . . . For us there is no cause of Jesus; only the cause of God exists for us.

—Martin Buber's Memorial
Address for Leonard Ragaz
as cited by Ernst Simon,
Jewish Frontier,
February 1948.

*B*uber's vision of mutuality has relevance beyond the three spheres of nature, the interhuman, and aesthetic forms in which "I-Thou" may be spoken by one being to another. The philosophy of relation provides a perspective which one may take toward social realities as well. It provides the basis upon which we may transcend the stark choice which Kierkegaard posed as the existential possibility of the nineteenth century, between the authentic life of the single one and the life of the collective in which personal life collapses and is subsumed in the life of the party, the crowd. The alternative Buber envisioned is life in the community, in which human beings have essentially to do with one another, but in such a way that the personal life of all is enhanced and nourished, not diminished. This approach also extends to seeing ways in which communities may live cooperatively alongside one another, rather than competitively and antagonistically. The relation of the Jewish and Arab communities in Palestine occupied Buber's heart and energy with special passion from the time he moved to Jerusalem in 1938 to his death in 1965. The relation of the Jewish and Christian communities is also one to which Buber devoted much attention, but in a less well-known and very different way. In this chapter I seek to show how Buber's understanding of Jesus as the Jewish brother can help to transform the relation of the Jewish and Christian communities. Contemporary Christian theologians, such as Rosemary Radford Ruether[1] and Paul Van Buren,[2] are showing us how faulty Christologies perpetuate misunderstanding and enfeeble the possibilities for genuine mutuality or dialogue between the two traditions. Their project is anticipated and finds needed support from the Jewish side in Buber's sympathetic assessment of the religious significance of Jesus.

_____

Jesus is the great divide. If Jew and Christian are ever to walk together and witness in harmony to the world, it will be as they link arms with Jesus the common brother. Roman Catholic and Protestant rapprochement becomes possible as both gain a transformed regard for Martin Luther. In much the same way, Jewish and Christian confraternity is importantly deepened as both gain a transformed regard for Jesus, the "great Nazarene,"[3] through whom "something from the innermost center of Israel, however modified,"[4] penetrated into the Gentile world. Buber can help us recover just what that "something" was.

Buber's "open-minded"[5] attitude toward Jesus is well known. Karl Thieme felt that he had "gone as far as a Jew could go in honouring Jesus of Nazareth."[6] Honoring and appreciating the man from Galilee do not, of course, "make one a Christian." Such adverting, nonetheless, contributed to the kind of impact that Buber had upon contemporary Christian thought, an influence which Malcolm Diamond perceived was behind the charge by some that Buber was a "crypto-Christian."[7] He clearly is, in John Bennett's words, a startling reminder of just "how much of the Christian content of that faith is possible without an acceptance of the Christian mediation."[8] It is not, of course, Jesus in his ostensible Christian significance that is central for Buber, but Jesus in his Jewishness, Jesus in that aspect of his existence that has been bracketed so long by so many Christians and opposed by so many Jews. For all of his sympathy toward Jesus, a sympathy which made even his own Jewishness suspect in some quarters, Buber remained what he called an "arch Jew," one who was such through and through, from the original covenant. As he wrote to Gandhi, ". . . although I should not have been among the crucifiers of Jesus, I should also not have been among his supporters."[9] It is precisely as this arch Polish Jew *qua* Jew that Buber identified, attended to, and loved Jesus as a Jewish brother.

Most interpreters of Buber have noted his lifetime preoccupation with the New Testament and with the Christian faith.[10] Its peculiar tone was set early when, as a young man of about twenty-three, he read Schweitzer's essay on the Eucharist. "This essay," Buber commented later, "made a deep impression on me because it brought Jesus into close relation with the mysteries of Jewish faith."[11] This interpretation of Jesus in relation to Judaism made it natural for Buber to link together "Moses, the prophets, and Jesus"[12] and to evaluate Jesus in terms of his relationship to Moses. Moses, Buber said, had ". . . a genius which could find its parallel only in Jesus. . . ."[13] Why, then, did not Buber choose Moses rather than Jesus as a paradigm of a person in pure relation with God in *I and Thou?*[14] Buber's critics were puzzled. Chaim Potok attributed this move to Buber's "early involvement with Christian mysticism"[15] which, he claimed, "remained a dominant factor in Buber's thinking and colored his later understanding of Judaism."[16] Such an interpretation fails to appreciate Buber's quite radical departure, after *Daniel,* from the paradigm of mystical unity and its fundamental categories, and his acceptance of the ineradicable Jewishness of Jesus. Buber considered himself a "brother" of Jesus, and as a brother felt that he could know Jesus from within "in the impulses and stirring of his Jewish being, in a way that remains inaccessible to the peoples submissive to him."[17]

Buber's most moving and eloquent testimony on his subject comes from the opening pages of *Two types of Faith,* his most ambitious and sustained analysis of New Testament texts:

> From my youth onwards I have found in Jesus my great brother. That Christianity has regarded and does regard him as God and Saviour has always appeared to me a fact of the highest importance which, for his sake and my own, I must endeavor to understand. . . . My own fraternally open relationship to him has grown ever stronger and clearer, and today I see him more strongly and clearly than ever before.

I am more than ever certain that a great place belongs to him in Israel's history of faith and that this place cannot be described by any of the usual categories. . . .[18]

I regard this Jewish endorsement of "Jesus as brother" a recognition of the highest possible significance for the self-understanding of both Judaism and Christianity, and for the contribution that their encounter thus enriched might make to our common well-being. Traditional Jewish critics, such as Alexander Kohanski,[19] suggest otherwise. They regard Buber's interpretations of Jesus as "legitimate standpoints of Christianity but not of Judaism," and find Buber's view of the ministry of Jesus to be "entirely personal on his part. . . ."[20] The failure to deal with the positive import for Buber of viewing Jesus as brother leads an Orthodox or Traditional reader to be unduly sensitive to finding Christian nuances in Buber where there are none, and "finding" them to reject Buber's approach as assimilationist in implication. Beginning with Buber's view of Jesus as brother is the conceptual move that helps to interpret "Jewishly," as it were, Buber's other references to Jesus. These references are of three kinds, each in connection with one of three basic aspects of Jewish faith: the teaching about God, about faith, and about messianism. In each of these aspects Buber distinguishes a genuinely Jewish way of regarding Jesus from a Christianized way. I will try to suggest how the image of Jesus as brother helps to keep Buber's conclusions from being personal in an eccentric or idiosyncratic sense, and opens up their programmatic importance.

Jesus as a Fulfilled Man but Not the Fulfillment

The special character of Buber's incorporation of Jesus into the history and faith of Judaism is based, in the first instance, upon Buber's perception of the fundamental Jewish teaching about God. Jesus is a prophet of the Kingship of God, in the fullest and purest relationship to God, but is not himself God, nor an incarnation of God, since God neither needs nor is capable of being represented, or mediated, or imaged. Thus, *Jesus is a fulfilled man, but not the fulfillment.* The fundamental Jewish teaching about God, according to Buber, is not the abstract concept of one God rather than and over against many gods—although this is certainly involved. Nor is the fundamental teaching about God an ethical or an ethicized monotheism, although this view of God clearly sanctions a particular moral picture of human existence in the world. The fundamental teaching about the one God is basically a qualitative, not a quantitative, matter.[21]

> The great deed of Israel is not that it taught the one real God, who is the origin and goal of all being, but that it pointed out that this God can be addressed by man in reality, that man can say Thou to Him, that he can stand face to face with Him, that he can have intercourse with Him.[22]

This God is imageless, but can be known and addressed in the world. Yet God as such is unseen, not given over to the world of the senses, yet "speaks to man in the things and beings that He sends him in life."[23] It is there, in our relation to the concrete actualities of just these things and beings, that we are to answer God. Thus "the real communion of man with God not only has its place in the world, but also its subject."[24]

An essential aspect of Moses' greatness is the vigor of his opposition to the tendency "to reduce the Divinity to a form available for and identifiable by the senses,"[25] a tendency present in every religion that stems from the meeting of a human person and the mystery of God. What Moses established was the principle "of the imageless presence of the invisible, who permits Himself to be seen."[26] But these permissions (the many anthropomorphisms, so to speak, of the Hebrew Scriptures) do not qualify the unseen, the imageless nature of God as such.[27] They are temporary openings, permissions, never embodiments or incarnations. The New Testament and Christian faith do speak of Jesus as the "image of God" (Col. 1:15; 2

Cor. 4:4), as one who represents God "in the image of a human being and a human life."[28] Such a mediating figure is, however, for Buber, alien to what he has in mind when he speaks of coming to the unseeable God through the things and beings of the world. Together with the idea of fate, the idea of a mediator different in nature from the occasional intervention of earthly and heavenly powers is a penetration into Jewish Hellenism which begins to compromise the Mosaic revelation. There have been tendencies throughout Jewish history to reduce the invisibility of God. (It is that reductionistic function, rather than anything forensic, which is at the heart of Buber's references here to "mediator.") But each of these tendencies has fallen short of what Buber calls the Christian route of "deification."

> Neither the *logos* of Philo nor the pre-existent heavenly being of the book of Enoch is a mediator in the christological sense, but each of them indicates a tendency towards it.[29]

The *zaddik* of the Hasidic tales which Buber retold with such insight was perhaps a sort of mediator, a kind of "midwife of the divine Spirit,"[30] living in both worlds and yet the connecting link between them. The *zaddik* did indeed perform such a function, but insofar as he was successful he compromised the audaciousness of the Mosaic disclosure. "The *zaddik*," wrote Buber, as he gave new voicing to the tales of Rabbi Nachman, "made the Hasidic community richer in security of God, but poorer in the one thing of value—one's own seeking."[31] Authentic Jewish religiousness must, then, be on guard against the tendency to hallow the *zaddik,* instead of hallowing life itself. The holiness of the holy man is not his possession or permanent quality as such, but is rather his clear witness to the addressability of God. If this is the case with the *zaddikim* of Hasidism, it is true, a *fortiori,* of Jesus of Nazareth.

Buber finds Jesus to be the paradigm, the prototypical representative of the fulfilled person in relation to God, but one who himself is not the end, the fulfillment, the accomplished work, the completion. Jesus appears in *I and Thou* as this unified, or "fulfilled man." Socrates speaks the I of unending dialogue between human beings. Goethe speaks the I of pure communion with nature. But Jesus speaks the I of unconditioned relation with the Eternal Thou, calling his Thou "Father." Jesus speaks thus out of the solidarity of relation, as a genuinely "fulfilled" man. This is to be set as sharply as possible over against the illusory fulfillment of the self-asserting Napoleon (who spoke the "I" but "without the power to enter into relation"), and the equally illusory fulfillment envisioned in the absorptionist mysticism of Buddhism.[32] With Jesus we do not have to do, so to speak, with the cause of Jesus, but only and always with the cause of God. We do not begin to get Jesus as mediator until "the unity of the teaching is translated from lived life to content and form."[33]

In a wholly Jewish proclamation Jesus teaches that every person could become a child of God by living unconditionally.[34] But this teaching is not knowledge as such, but a "Way and a lived revelation."[35] In Jesus (as in the Buddha and Lao-tzu), Buber "met with truth that is lived and transmitted, the fulfilling man who is himself teaching," whose way is not his but God's,[36] which is exemplified in the free deed and not the prescribed service. This kind of truth has more to do with life and practice than with the knowledge of being, for it is capable of being "handed down from generation to generation as a way of life."[37] In relation, then, to the fundamental Jewish teaching about God, Jesus appears as the unified, central, or "fulfilled man," and as such is well within the bounds of Judaism. He is a witness to the one who remains Thou, and as such is "brother," not mediator. Guides, messengers, prophets are possible for they do not compromise the unseeable God. But this "Jewish world of belief, which knows no god but God" collapses with the testimony of Thomas that the Risen One is indeed "My Lord and My God," and who by virtue of this testimony becomes, among all the disciples of Jesus, the first Christian in the sense of the Christian dogma.[38]

Jesus as a Man of Faith but Not an Object of Faith

The special character of Buber's incorporation of Jesus into the history and faith of Judaism is based, in the second instance, upon Buber's analysis of the nature of faith. Thus, *Jesus is a man of faith but not an object of faith.* This picturing of the options of faith is found in Buber's New Testament study, *Two Types of Faith.* The possibilities are twofold and no more: the Hebraic *emunah* or the Greek *pistis*; the Jewish "unconditional trust" or the Christian "accepting and recognizing as true of a proposition pronounced about the object of faith."[39] Jesus under the figure of *emunah* is the Jewish brother, the man of faith, the one who finds himself in an unconditional relation of trust in God. This, Buber asserts, is the Jesus of the genuine tradition,[40] the Jesus who trusts and believes. Jesus under the figure of *pistis* is the Christianized Jesus, the one whose reticence and declination to make himself an object of cult and belief has been overcome.[41] This, Buber asserts, is the Jesus of theology, the Jesus of the Pauline and Johannine construction, the Jesus about whom credal affirmations are made. All language about Jesus as believer is the Jewish witness to a brother; all language about Jesus as God is the Greek gospel about a prodigal. The difference is not simply a shift in perspective, a different way of looking at the same event. The difference follows from a radical shift of faith from its Jewish sense to it Greek sense.

Although faith to Buber is unconditional trust and not assent to putative proposition (a distinction which he finds at the heart of Jesus' teaching),[42] it does not follow that such trust or faith (*emunah*) is contentless. It clearly does not have the objective principle(s) of *pistis,* nor, as Friedman observes, is it the phenomenological analysis of existence, much less a matter of 'having' experiences. "It is rather the wholly particular content of each moment of lived dialogue in which the reality one meets is neither subjectivized nor objectivized but *responded to.*"[43] The transformation of Jesus into an object of belief or faith, then, follows the same logic as the transformation of Jesus from the fulfilled one who addresses God into Jesus who is addressed in God's place.

> Jesus, not certainly, the actual man Jesus, but the image of Jesus as it entered into the soul of the peoples and transformed it—allows God to

be addressed only in conjunction with himself, the Christ. Only as borne along by him, the Logos, can the human word now penetrate to Him who is the origin and goal of all being; the "way" to the Father now goes only through him.[44]

Here, as in the first instance, Jesus could be regarded in a genuinely Jewish fashion as one of the beings given to us in the world who witnesses to the immediacy and the addressability of God. But again, as in the first instance, regarding Jesus as an incarnation, a mediator, an embodiment in a sensibly accessible way is an un-Jewish and idolatrous abridgement of the mystery of God. Jesus as *emunah* invites us to look where he looks; Jesus as *pistis* invites us to look at him. This point is made with special sharpness in Buber's comment on Jesus' deflection of faith in himself: "There is none good, but God alone" (Mark 10:17).

No theological interpretation can weaken the directness of this statement. Not only does it continue the great line of the Old Testament proclamation of the non-humanity of God and the non-divinity of man in a special way, which is distinguished by the personal starting-point and the point of reference; against the tendencies toward deification of the post-Augustan ecumeny, its thirst after becoming a god and making gods, it also opposes the fact of remaining man.[45]

A corollary of the *emunah-pistis* polarity makes even clearer for Buber the authentic Jewishness of the former and the peculiar Christianness of the latter; this concerns the relationship of each picture of faith to the notion of community. "The origin of the Jewish *emunah* is in the history of a nation, that of the Christian *pistis* in that of individuals."[46] As representative of *emunah*, then, Jesus is clearly brother in a way impossible for Jesus as representative of *pistis*. As the latter the one-time brother would be wrenched from his family and be regarded as either its destroyer or the transcender, one who has new brothers and sisters made for him to replace the brothers and sisters who were his natural gift. Now *emunah* and *pistis* are not exhaustively found in any particular religious tradition, but each does have its representative actuality, in Judaism and Christianity respectively. Buber's point is not, however, that there is community in Judaism and only individuals in Christianity. His point is, rather, that the basis of the community has been changed. Founded on *emunah,* community is given; founded on *pistis,* community is created. One 'finds oneself in' faith as *emunah;* one is 'converted to ' faith as *pistis.* Buber holds that Jesus and the prophets did indeed have a common message— "the turning of man and the Kingship of God."[47] But the Christian insistence upon regarding Jesus under the figure of *pistis* rather than *emunah* led it to picture Jesus as demanding that one should "live as though the Kingdom of God had already dawned," and so no longer affirming "the people as such."[48]

> The action of Christianity at the time of her separation from Judaism, involved forsaking . . . the idea of the holiness of the nation and the absolute value of its task. . . . The kingdom of God in the eyes of Christianity means the establishment of God's Kingdom over the redeemed souls in the world, in which there is no longer a relation between the nation as a nation and God; therefore, people become Christians only as individuals, but the nations as nations remained idol worshippers. . . .[49]

The possibility of regarding Jesus as brother is not something which Buber sought to do in order to act against Christianity for its theological distortion of the Galilean prophet of God's Kingship. He hoped that such a recovery might be a move in the direction of overcoming the opposition of the two communities, and reconciling the antinomy of trust and credal faith. He hoped, for example, that in the revival of Jewish life in the ancient homeland Israel might become a mediating model community for fusing the spirit of east and west into a unity.[50]

> The faith of Judaism and the faith of Christendom are by nature different in kind, each in conformity with its human basis, and they will indeed remain different, until mankind is gathered in from the exiles of the "religions" into the Kingship of God. But an Israel striving after the renewal of its faith through the rebirth of the person and a Christianity striving for the renewal of its faith through the rebirth of nations would have something as yet unsaid to say to each

other and a help to give to one another—hardly to be conceived at the present time.[51]

Jesus as a Messianic Man but Not the Messiah

The special character of Buber's incorporation of Jesus into the history and faith of Judaism is based, in the third instance, upon his analysis of Hebraic messianism. Thus, *Jesus is a messianic man but not the Messiah*. Two of the principal forms which the figure of the *Mashiach* of Israel had taken in the pre-Christian period were the pre-exilic form of the king, and the exilic form of the prophetic servant.[52] Both forms were intrinsically related to the Hebraic vision of the continuity between the creating and redeeming acts of God; both presuppose that "the Messianic man is . . . an ascending and not a descending one."[53] But in either form the messianic person is a recurring figure. Hebraic messianism required continuity.[54] "It is a mistake," said Buber, "to regard Jewish Messianism as a belief in an event happening once at the end of time and in a single human figure created as the center of this event."[55] Thus the Jewish vision of redemption, and its Hasidic expression in particular, is opposed to any sense of the self-differentiation "of one man from other men, of one time from other times, of one act from other actions."[56]

There are two dimensions to this interpretation of messianism, one of which reveals Jesus-as-brother as a messianic man, and one of which shows Jesus as a messianic pretender, an announced Messiah, one in the line extending through Sabbatai Zvi to Jacob Frank. The first aspect is the servant form of genuine messianic vocation; the second aspect is its silence or hiddenness. These dimensions are interwoven and cannot easily be separated. They can, however, be distinguished in connection with their relation to Jesus.

> In my view the life history of Jesus is not to be understood unless we realize that he stood within the shadow of the servant of Yahweh in Deutero-Isaiah (as Christian theologians, especially Albert Schweitzer, have also pointed out). But he left the concealment of the quiver (Isaiah 49:2), while the "holy Jew" remained within it.[57]

Chaim Potok understand Buber to be saying that God's servant is to suffer in silence, "without knowing his role in the messianic scheme of things. It is his task to wait until such time as God draws him forth to proclaim his messianic nature to the world."[58] Jesus' violation of this condition is an aberration, but not so serious as to separate him from the fraternal life of his people. The break with Judaism as Buber sees it,

> . . . comes not with him [Jesus] but with Paul, who made the man who suffers for the work of Yahweh into the God who suffers for the sake of men.[59]

From that moment on, the paths of Judaism and Christianity separated. The decisive point is not that the Messiah must suffer; rather that, as an expression of the concealment or secrecy that is essential to the servant's identity, he simply accepts the suffering which comes his way.[60]

> This Messianic mystery rest upon the hiddenness; not upon a secret attitude, but upon a genuine, factual hiddenness reaching into the innermost existence. The men through whom it passes are those of whom the nameless prophet speaks when he says, in the first person, that God sharpens them to a polished arrow and then conceals them in His quiver. Their hiddenness belongs to the essence of their work of sufffering. Each of them can be the fulfilling one; none of them in his self-knowledge may be anything other than a servant of the Lord. With the tearing apart of the hiddenness not only would the work itself be suspended, but a counter work would be set up. Messianic self-disclosure is the bursting of Messiahship.[61]

Buber suggests that Jesus is a messianic man under the shadow or model of the servant of God, but his self-identification as Messiah (or the church's identification of him as Messiah) negated the possibility of his serving a genuinely messianic or servant function for Israel. The church interpreted Jesus' suffering as the decisive once-for-all event; but for Judaism such a decisive event takes place at all times, in every here and now.[62] The church finds Jesus to be a rupture in God's creative-redemptive action in the world; Judaism insists on an unbroken continuity of human history. This sense of no irruption of the historical line, together with the teaching of the possibility of the immediate relationship to God, that is, the nonincarnation of God, are the decisive factors constituting the ultimate division between Judaism and Christianity.[63]

> What is decisive is not the conception of redemption itself; this already lived in prophetic Messianism and was developed by post-exilic Judaism to the core of its world view. But to the saviour religious redemption is a fact — one by its nature transcending history, nonetheless localized in it; to Judaism it is a pure prospect. For Christianity the historical age (''the present aeon'') has a caesura, an absolute center in which, as it were, it erupts, until the ground is split open. . . . For Judaism history, without any such central mooring point and left entirely to its never-ceasing flow, must strive for ''the end.''[64]

Thus, in this third instance, as in the first two, Jesus can be regarded in a genuinely Jewish fashion, in which he returns as a genuine brother to all the sons and daughters of Israel. This is Jesus as a messianic man, but not the Messiah. Jesus is a man of faith but not an object of faith. Jesus is a fulfilled man but not the fulfillment. The brother may be a witness but only insofar as he does not call attention to himself.

> In order really to understand the relation of Judaism to the appearance of Jesus, one must descend into the depths of this faith, which is not condensed in any creed but can be shown from the testimonies. Whatever the appearance of Jesus means for the Gentile world (and its significance for the Gentile world remains for me the true seriousness of Western history), seen from the standpoint of Judaism he is the first in the series of men who, stepping out of the hiddenness of the servant of the Lord, the real ''Messianic mystery,'' acknowledged their Messiahship in their souls and in their words. That this first one in the series was imcomparably the purest, the most legitimate, the most endowed with real Messianic power — as I experience ever again when those personal words that ring true to me merge for me into a unity whose speaker becomes visible to me — alters nothing in the fact of this firstness; indeed it undoubtedly belongs just to it, to the fearfully penetrating reality that has characterized the whole automessianic series.[65]

Any evaluation of Buber's fraternal viewing of Jesus that regards it as being grounded on more than "personal, psychological considerations"[66] must note briefly several of the areas in which most New Testament scholarship would now not support much of what he says. Some of his conclusions and points of departure must be corrected or modified.

(1) Most scholars no longer draw the contrast between Paul and Jesus or between Paul and Judaism so sharply as Buber does. Increasingly the tendency has been to find Jewish sources for much of Paul's teaching.[67]

(2) Buber sought to account for the contrast between the Synoptic and Johannine pictures of Jesus and the contrast between Paul and Jesus by a hermeneutic that appealed to the hellenization of either Judaism or the gospel. This theory has now largely been either abandoned or radically modified in recent years. Much that Buber thought was late and Greek in the Gospel narratives has now been shown to be early and Jewish—and the latter not of the Hellenistic diaspora, but of a genuine Palestinian provenance. This is one of the 'assured results' of the vast research achieved to date on the Qumran material. We now know that Jewish religiousness at the time of Jesus was a far more variegated phenomenon than Buber believed. As Gerald Sloyan observed in his early essay on "Buber and the Significance of Jesus," the "Warriors of light, the men of Qumran have thus returned to destroy many a liberal hypothesis."[68]

(3) In his legitimate reclamation for Judaism of Jesus in his Jewishness, Buber has gone beyond the evidence in suggesting that "the religious sphere within which Jesus lived and moved was that of the Talmud and Midrash," that is, within the circle of belief characterized by Pharisaic Judaism.[69] Buber rightly observed that the teaching of Jesus that is "preserved" in the New Testament, sometimes in several and different forms, is to be understood by using the clues provided by the Jewish culture that Jesus breathed and interpreted. His metaphors and idioms and his interests and goals are explicable only with respect to their Jewish and Palestinian milieu. In addition, many of his

teachings, in their form and their content, can now be seen as either paralleling or being drawn from other contemporaneous rabbinic teaching. Indeed, the richer we find the Judaism of Jesus' day to be, the more deeply rooted we find his own faith-structure to be in things Jewish. Unless "the intention of the Torah" be seen as "a matter of intense and unconditional concern"[70] for Jesus, his views are impenetrable. On the other hand, Jesus' originality persists. For all of Buber's Jewish location of Jesus' time and space, the creative and novel aspects of his teaching and of his religious views remain untouched. The analysis of such scholars as Jeremias reminds us that we can get back to some characteristic patterns of Jesus' teaching, and that we find here elements of a unique claim to authority and a sense of a unique relationship to God.[71] Jesus teaches that God loves even those who are not able to understand themselves as prepared or as preparable for that love. The peculiar nature of his teaching is seen not simply by posing his words over against the speech of his contemporaries; it is most clearly visible in his behavior, his pattern of acting. Here we find not only an unconventional openness to all sorts and conditions of persons, most dramatically women—as friends, companions, conversation partners, recipients of his affection and ministry—but also a view of the possibilities of God's relation to humanity that was genuinely subversive of the Temple establishment. For all of Buber's discovery of Jesus' Jewishness, there is simply too much that bursts out of the constraints of these categories.

(4) But the most serious reservation to Buber's approach[72] is his assumption that the historical Jesus, Jesus as he really was, is both distinguishable from Jesus as he was believed to be and recoverable as such in considerable detail. Diamond has surely exaggerated the case in his claim that "Buber has emerged as one of the most trenchant critics of the understanding of Jesus as the 'Christ of Faith,' the central figure of Trinitarian Christianity."[73] But it is still true that Buber seems to depend in his analysis on the ability to separate out the "faith of Jesus" from the "faith about Jesus," to find the real Jesus after peeling off the Pauline and Johannine overlays. Again, the

thrust of contemporary New Testament scholarship is now
nearly unanimous in maintaining that the distinction between
the historical Jesus and the kerygmatic Christ can have only a
preliminary usefulness, and that all of the apostolic literature is
written in and reflects the prespective of belief in and about
Jesus. The New Testament might accurately be subtitled "the
faith of the early Christian community," for nowhere do we have
fact ranged over against interpretation, or *emunah* free from
pistis. We can still, I maintain, hear the voice of Jesus, but that
task requires a much different kind of hermeneutic from the sort
in which Buber was prepared to engage. It is not quite so easy as
he thought to set a Synoptic Jesus over against Paul and John.
But if Buber is wrong and needs to be corrected or modified, it is
for the sort of consideration suggested here, and not for the
reasons that some of his Jewish critics have suggested.

Professor Kohanski, for example, does not believe that
Buber's search for the original, the historical, Jesus is a vain
search, but is convinced that the real Jesus which Buber finds is
not Jewish after all, except in a trivial, perhaps ethnic sense.
This view seems to suggest that the Judaism for which Buber
reclaims Jesus is not really authentic Judaism, that we should
expect Buber to find this non-Jewish Jesus to his liking since
both of them opt for spontaneity over structure, for attitude over
law, and for trust over obedience.[74] The familiar Orthodox
judgment of Buber was that he was not fully or authentically
Jewish. That Buber was not halachically Jewish was no secret.
But Buber thought it possible to be "nonobservant," as it were,
and still to be religiously Jewish; indeed, for him, he thought it
the only possibility. The Orthodox verdict is that this was a
contradiction and an impossibility, the final subjectivization of
the Mosaic revelation. But Judaism becomes normatively
rabbinic (and halachic?) only in the period following the
cessation of sacrifice in the Temple on July 17, 70 (for the first
time since the return from exile) and following the complete
destruction of the sanctuary by Titus on August 6th of the same
year. The Zealots had been decimated; the Essenes and
Covenanters, moved to the periphery; the Sadducees, discredit-

ed. Only the Pharisaic party had the resources upon which a new integration of Judaism could be based.[75] Even if one were to regard this Yavneh settlement as legislating for subsequent Jewish generations (in which case Buber's Judaism would be considered marginal and personal), it is surely not legitimate to read it backwards into the time of Jesus and to use it as the measure against which the Jesus of the New Testament (in all strata) is found to be not only insufficiently Jewish, but also and pervasively a Christian Jesus. Even modified, Buber is surely correct in his essential emphasis on the Jewishness of Jesus. Without that Jewishness being as deeply rooted as possible, the Christian dogma of incarnation is severely questioned. The human nature held to be assumed by God in that act was fully human in its Jewish particularity, whatever else Christians may want and need to say about it. As James Muilenberg observed, Buber ". . . is the best contemporary corrective to the persistent Marcionism of large segments of the Christian Church."[76]

Christians will want to affirm, over against Buber, the originality of Jesus, his creative transformation of Jewish ideas, including that of Messiahship. Christians will want to acknowledge the synonymity of the Risen Christ with the Historical Jesus, and to evaluate positively the refounding of God's people evident in his words and deeds. Christians will want to insist that in their faith and cultus God indeed is spoken to, not just spoken about. But all of this will be done in a more chastened, less arrogant manner in the light of Buber's embracing of his brother Jesus, a fulfilled messianic man of faith. It may not be too much to hope that some kinds of Christological exuberance might be considerably sobered were Christians also to find that one whom they call both Lord and God to be their brother as well.

Buber's most moving credo needs, finally, to be heard by those who find his brother Jesus insufficiently Jewish and by those who find him to be insufficiently Christian. This eloquent testimony follows upon Buber's 1926 discussion of Peter's confession of Jesus of Nazareth to be the Christ, the confession which Mark (8:27-30) located as having occurred at Caesarea Philippi at the beginning of Jesus' Synoptic pligrimage to

Jerusalem:

> I believe something was said in Caesarea Philippi that was well and
> truly intended, and yet was not true, and the fact that it has been
> repeated down the centuries still does not make it true. I believe that
> God reveals himself not in people, but only *through* them. I believe
> that the *Mashiach* does not come at a paricular moment in history;
> his coming can only be the end of history. I believe that the world's
> redemption did not become a fact nineteen centuries ago. We are still
> living in a world that is not redeemed; we are still looking forward to
> the redemption—and each of us is called to do his part in the work of
> redeeming the world. Israel is the community of people which retains
> this purely messianic expectation, even though the Jews have all too
> often proved unfaithful to it. That is what Israel always is, what she
> will be to the end; and because she has her part in the work of accom-
> plishing the end, Israel must sustain her faith in the coming of the
> kingdom—that is, a faith that the world is not as yet redeemed and
> that the redemption must come. In our faith, in the faith of Israel, the
> redemption of the world is one and the same with the finishing of
> creation. The man who raises Jesus to so high a place ceases to be one
> of us, and if he wants to challenge our faith that the redemption lies in
> the future . . . then we go our separate ways. [77]

Christians, too, look to a redemptive future, and not just to a
redemptive past. The contrast between Jewish and Christian
ways of living with respect to the future may not be so distinct or
so unambiguous as Buber claims. [78] But neither Christian nor
Jew will be able to look at that past or anticipate that future in the
conventional way after accepting Buber's invitation to come,
stand with him, and look together at Jesus, the common Jewish
brother, the fulfilled messianic man of faith. [79]

IV. The Vision

I have no teaching. I only point to something. I point to reality. I point to something in reality that had not or had too little been seen. I take him who listens to me by the hand and lead him to the window. I open the window and point to what is outside. I have no teaching, but I carry on a conversation.

— Martin Buber, "Replies to My Critics"

We have examined in some detail and in distinction from each other three facets of the thought of Martin Buber which have seemed to many readers to be puzzling, problematic, or peripheral and eccentric—the sphere of nature, the life of the helper, and the figure of Jesus. It is our concern in these concluding pages to set these inquiries in relation to one another, and to suggest how Buber's vision of mutuality encompasses and integrates these three subjects.

The task before us in this chapter is twofold: (1) to show that Buber's embracing of Jesus as his Jewish brother, and by extension, his pointing out a direction for Jewish-Christian relations, is an appropriate application of his central insight; and (2) to identify explicitly that dimension of mutuality which informs and connects the three subjects which we have explored. Each side of this two-fold task is occasioned by questions which arise from the conclusions many readers have drawn, frequently and without warrant, from that relation which Buber uses as the paradigm of mutuality— the interhuman situation of two human beings.

(1) There is no question that Buber's model of personal reciprocity is the encounter of two human beings—each of whom confirms the other, meets and steps into relation with the other. Buber devoted most of his energies to a careful phenomenological analysis and elucidation of just such an encounter; further, there is no gainsaying the fact that this choice provides the sort of illuminating power required of a model or paradigm case. Mutuality is most fully and clearly disclosed when two individuals speak ''Thou'' to one another.

This reciprocal turning of one person toward another exposes the heart of mutuality, but the question is whether or not this picture is applicable as well to wider ranges of the interhuman in such a way as to be equally evocative. Can the vision of mutuality derived from the meeting of two individuals shed sufficient light on the possibilities for the genuine meeting of human communities, such as the social realities of the Jewish and Christian traditions? We are not thinking here of the theoretical or doctrinal relations between two 'religions' or theological systems; nor are we asking how Buber's vision of mutuality might lend some clarity and help to overcome the alleged conflict between two structures of belief, two competing sets of truth claims about the relation of God and the human sphere. That conceptual task is neither impossible nor unimportant. Our concern, however, is with the societies, the communities of men and women whose associations and disengagements evidence a complex and painful history. These communities are, of course, characterized by distinctive ways of believing, but our emphasis should be on the communities themselves rather than the theological affirmations and histories which both connect and divide them, but do not exhaustively define them.

Some have argued that the complexities of these social lives are such as to preclude any successful application of the way of mutuality to the sphere of relations between or among peoples and larger social groups. The contention is that the way of mutuality is inapplicable to social and political structures since only one person can speak "Thou" to one other person. This objection, however, as natural as it may appear, rests upon a fundamental error. It confuses principle with procedures, confuses the idea of applying the concept of mutuality to the larger social situations with the manner or mode(s) of such an application. Reinhold Niebuhr's influential view about the relation of religious understanding to social ethics was noted for its realistic analysis of the possibilities of human community in the light of a particular view of human nature that recognized continuing human sinfulness, especially in societies. For Niebuhr, when the philosophy of dialogue is extended to organized groups and nations, it becomes utopian romanticism. Paul Pfuetze, an early American interpreter of Buber, felt, on different grounds, that Buber's approach simply could not be applied directly or practically to large-scale situations. Now there is no question that it is much easier to see the relevance of the way of mutuality to the sphere of the interhuman when only two individuals are involved, than to any other sphere. But there is no necessary contradiction in making such a move. Just as there are 'degrees' of mutuality, real if not full, that are possible in the sphere of nature, so there are 'degrees' of mutuality, real if not full, that are possible when groups of human beings move toward each other. These possibilities are diminished when that encounter is prefaced or its future prejudged by a theology of original sin (Niebuhr) or by bondage to a prior history of distrust, suspicion, and animosity.

The communal realm, the realm of the *polis,* the coming-to-be-of community, is precisely the realm in which the renewal of human life is to occur for Buber. The life of the individuals in the two-person paradigm is not abstracted from the concrete location of men and women in the social world. The recovery of personal meaning is in and through involvement with the things and beings of the world, not by withdrawing from community. We do not have to choose between being the single one and being lost in the crowd. Fully personal life is always life in community. Everything depends on the way in which mutuality, the dialogic, is applied to the communal situation of men and women. This is no less the case when that situation is the encounter of two communities each of which has an explicit religious dimension, in this case, the possibilities in the encounter between the Jewish and Christian communities wherever they find themselves open to engagement, open to having to do essentially with one another.

Martin Buber was convinced of the need to change what he called the real life of "man to man." The fact that the fulness of mutuality is most clearly seen in the meeting of two individuals who become authentic "persons" in their encounter never obscured for him the conviction that there were in our communal

life latent "possibilities of a right order" of mutuality.[1] He
worked to establish contacts that might allow those possibilities
to unfold, by seeking ways, for example, in which Jew and Arab
might live together in the common land of their inheritance, and
by pointing Jew and Christian to a life together devoid of
hesitation and triumphalism. He continually urged upon his
fellows that they open themselves to the risk, the danger, and
the surprise that go with dialogue. One does not so much apply
the way of dialogue to the meeting of human communities; one
seeks, rather, to let genuine dialogue unfold as it may.

The perspective or philosophy of mutuality is not a program
of social or communal relations, but it can alert societies—large
and diverse, small and familial—to sponsor those arrangements
of life and work out of which the fully human can emerge. The
community, the real living together of men and women with one
another, thrives, Buber said, "only when people have the real
things of their common life in common; where they can
experience, discuss and administer them together . . ."[2] For
Buber the best example of such a communal future was the
Israeli *kibbutz*, which he called "an experiment that did not
fail."[3] Participants in a *kibbutz* may draw near to one another as
they confront the work which they share. In a similar way, Jew
and Arab may draw near to one another in the boroughs and
quarters of Jerusalem as they confront the land which they
share. Again, Jew and Christian may draw near to one another
as they confront the figure of Jesus which they share. In the last
case, Buber's invitation to attend to the figure of Jesus as a
brother will help to reposition Jesus in the development of a
genuine Jewish religiousness, as well as to reassert Jesus'
Jewishness as an indispensable touchstone for Christian reflection, thus making communal dialogue in depth possible at last.

That there is a shared brother which grounds mutuality
between Jew and Christian is thus analogous to the educational
situation in which the shared text grounds mutuality between
teacher and pupil. The presence of this third factor in Jewish-
Christian dialogue, the great brother, is analogous as well to the
task or specified intention which occasions the encounter but

prevents the mutuality, while real, from becoming full in the three contexts discussed in Chapter Two—the educational, the therapeutic, and the sacramental situations.

(2) We have suggested that heeding Buber's call for the reciprocal recognition of Jesus as the common brother both facilitates genuine dialogue between Jews and Christians in their repective communities, and functions very much like a task which keeps that mutuality, while real, from reaching completeness. We are thus ready to identify explicitly that aspect of mutuality which informs and connects the three areas of this study. We begin, as always, with Buber's two-person paradigm of Thou-speaking. We saw how the centrality of that model led some readers to be uneasy about applying the vision of mutuality to the larger social sphere of communities and peoples. We have endeavored to suggest just how an awareness of the reciprocity present when two human beings step into relation with one another can illuminate the possibilities for reciprocity when communities that have been estranged and separated become open to moving toward each other.

In the same way we believe that only a misreading of the two-person paradigm would prevent one from discerning the common thread which runs through and ties together our investigation of the tree, the helper, and the brother. Since fulness of mutuality is possible only in the meeting of two individuals intending one another without reserve and without objectification, some have assumed that nothing like that mutuality is possible in any other sphere. What we have attempted to underscore, however, is the absolute importance and usefulness of working with Buber's insistence that there are "degrees" or "modes" of mutuality appropriate to all human contexts, not just the two-person encounter, that mutuality may be genuine and appropriate to the realities of any situation even when the givens of that situation do not make fulness possible.[4] The common theme of our analysis of Buber's vision, then, has been to lift up the dialectic of limitation and fulness, and to suggest the positive rather than the negative aspect of limitation. Some have thought that Buber's use of the two-person paradigm not only shows where mutuality happens but also prescribes where it may only happen. We have pointed out how that same paradigm can alert us to the authentic if limited mutuality that may occur whenever human beings have essentially to do with the things and beings of the world. Thus there is a dimension of that two-person mutuality which is clearly appropriate in our encounter with nature, in our task-oriented helping relationships, and in the openness of religiously based communities to one another. We take our cue from Buber himself who advised against prejudging where mutuality could or could not emerge, and who asks us to be ready and expecting wherever it does.

The limitation is different in each of our three studies, just as the mode of mutuality appropriate to the tree, the helper, and the brother is different. In the sphere of nature real mutuality is kept from being full by the inability of the mica, the tree, the cat, to have a world, to step over the threshold to us in faithful speech, although the closer the natural thing or being is to human freedom the fuller is the possibility of relation. In the sphere of interhuman helping contexts real mutuality is kept from being full by the inability of both partners to experience the relation from "the other side," to practice "inclusion." In the sphere of the encounter between the Jewish and Christian communities real mutuality is kept from being full by the long history of their "mis-meeting," a failure symbolized and effected by their common rejection of the Jewishness of Jesus. The differences among these limiting factors, thus, are of two kinds. The limitation in the sphere of nature and in the sphere of task-oriented interhuman relationships is irreducible, but the limitation in Jewish-Christian dialogue can be diminished as Jews and Christians find ways to incorporate Jesus in his Jewishness into their consciousness. An acceptance of Buber's picture of Jesus as the common brother can broaden Jews' appreciation of their ways of being religious, and can set a guard for Christians against their tendency toward a-historical Christological expression. For Jew and Christian to welcome Jesus as brother is once again to find themselves in the one family of God.

Our consideration of the brother, the helper, and the tree has shown the power and truth of Buber's vision. The limitation on the fulness of mutuality in each case affirms what is genuinely possible in the encounter and is a sign to us that we should not hesitate to step into a relation even when fulness may not be possible. We should regard the presence of a limit as the assurance of what may happen, rather than a declaration of what may not. All things may not be open to us, but with Buber's guidance we may be alerted to what has been neglected or obscured in our experience. With every melancholy there is exaltation; with every risk there is delight. In every relation, however partial, there is life. To stand with Buber at the window and to see as he helps us to see is to welcome "the grace that appears ever anew in earthly material,"[5] and to take that one step available that may help us to succeed at last in living with one another.

APPENDIX

Location of Buber's use of or reference to things and beings of the natural world according to the schema in the chart of this study:

I. *Zoological entities, at the threshold of mutuality*
1. beaver—"Distance and Relation," *The Knowledge of Man*, p. 62.
2. bird—"On Unity: Dialogue by the Sea," *Daniel*, p. 139.
3. butterfly—"The Teahing of the Tao," *Pointing the Way*, p. 51; *I and Thou* (trans. Kaufmann), p. 148, 69.
4. cat—*I and Thou* (trans. Kaufmann), p. 145.
5. cricket—"The Teaching of the Tao," *Pointing the Way*, p. 51.
6. dog—"Response to Willian Ernest Hocking," *Philosophical Interrogations*, p. 47.
7. horse—"Dialogue," *Between Man and Man*, pp. 22-23.
8. lion cub—*Between Man and Man*, pp. 1-3.
9. monkey—"Distance and Relation," *The Knowledge of Man*, pp. 64-65.
10. ox—"Distance and Relation," *Knowledge of Man*, pp. 60-61.
11. ram—"Distance and Relation," *Knowledge of Man*, pp. 60-61.

12. swallow—"Distance and Relation," *The Knowledge of Man*, pp. 60-61.
13. tuna—"Distance and Relation," *The Knowledge of Man*, pp. 60-61.

II. *Botanical entities, at the pre-threshold of mutuality*

14. flowers—"On Meaning: Dialogue in the Garden," *Daniel, p. 81.*
15. fruit—"Über Jacob Boehme," p. 253.
16. garden—"On Meaning: Dialogue in the Garden," *Daniel,* p. 81.
17. grain of seed—"On Unity: Dialogue by the Sea," *Daniel,* p. 135.
18. grass—"On Meaning: Dialogue in the Garden," *Daniel,* p. 81.
19. madrepores—"On Polarity: Dialogue after the Theater," *Daniel,* pp. 108-109.
20. mushrooms—"The Teaching of the Tao," *Pointing the Way,* p. 51.
21. thistle—"A Believing Humanism," *A Believing Humanism,* pp. 106-107.
22. linden/lime tree—"Man and His Image-Work," *The Knowledge of Man,* pp. 158-159. "Response to Helmut Kuhn," *Philosophical Interrogations,* p. 21.
23. oak tree—"Author's Preface," *Daniel,* p. 47.
24. olive tree—"A Believing Humanism," *A Believing Humanism,* pp. 106-107.
25. planted tree—"Distance and Relation," *The Knowledge of Man,* p. 62.
26. stone pine tree—"On Direction: Dialogue in the Mountains," *Daniel,* p. 54.
27. tree—"Über Jakob Boehme," p. 253.
28. tree—*I and Thou* (trans. Kaufmann), pp. 56-69; "What Is Man?" *Between Man and Man,* pp. 177-178.
29. wine—"Über Jakob Boehme," p. 253.

III. *The elements, at the subthreshold of mutuality*

30. air/breeze—"Über Jakob Boehme," p. 252.
31. air/wind—"On Unity: Dialogue by the Sea," *Daniel*, p. 128.
32. mica—"On Unity: Dialogue by the Sea," *Daniel*, pp. 140-141, pp. 142-143.
33. mica—*I and Thou* (trans. Kaufmann), pp. 146-147.
34. heap of stones—"A Believing Humansim," *A Believing Humanism*, pp. 106-107.
35. clump of earth—"Über Jakob Boehme," p. 253.
36. sandy plain—"On Polarity: Dialogue After the Theater," *Daniel*, pp. 108-109.
37. desert—"Man and His Image Work," *The Knowledge of Man*, p. 159.
28. sea—"On Unity: Dialogue by the Sea," *Daniel*, pp.131, 138, 127-138.
39. lake—"On Unity: Dialogue by the Sea," *Daniel*, p. 134.
40. tide—"On Unity: Dialogue by the Sea," *Daniel*, pp. 142-143.
41. waves—"On Polarity: Dialogue after the Theater," *Daniel*, pp. 108-109.
42. sun—"Über Jakob Boehme," p. 253.

NOTES

Preface

1. Martin Buber, "What is Man?," in *Between Man and Man*, (New York: Macmillan, 1965), p. 126.
2. Martin Buber, *I and Thou*, trans. Walter Kaufmann (New York: Charles Scribner's Sons, 1970), p. 85.
3. Martin Buber, "Education," in *Between Man and Man*, p. 88.
4. Buber, "What Is Man?" in *Between Man and Man*, p. 201.
5. Martin Buber, *Ich und Du* (Berlin: Schocken Verlag, 1936), p. 35.
6. J. H. Oldham, *Real Life Is Meeting* (New York: Sheldon Press, 1942), p. 28.
7. Martin Buber, *I and Thou*, trans. Ronald Gregor Smith (New York: Charles Scribner's Sons, 1958).
8. Walter Kaufmann, "Prologue to Martin Buber's *I and Thou*," pp. 14-15, 20-21, 38. In his discussion of Kaufmann's translation, Maurice Friedman points to an additional consideration that counts against the use of "You" for *Du*, namely the "already established usage of thirty-three years [by 1970; 47 years by 1984] and a whole literature in which 'I-Thou' is employed." *Martin Buber's Life and Work: The Early Years 1878—1923* (New York: E. P. Dutton, 1981), p. 429.

Chapter I

1. Martin Buber, *Ich und Du* (Berlin: Schocken Verlag, 1936), p. 13.
2. *I and Thou*, trans. Kaufmann, p. 77.

3. The third sphere of relation has to do with what Buber called ''geistige Wesenheiten,'' a phrase which has not fared well in English. In his first English translation, (1935), Ronald Gregor Smith suggested ''intelligible forms,'' revising it for the second edition (1957) as ''spiritual beings.'' That locution is not happier than its German original. Most people assumed that it would be changed in Walter Kaufmann's new translation (1970), particularly since much of Kaufmann's project was motivitated by a desire to cleanse Buber's classic from the nuance of Protestant piety whose distorting presence he claimed to find in Smith's earlier efforts. Indeed, Maurice Friedman had hoped for just such a ''correction.'' In his review of Robert Wood's book on Buber's ontology, Friedman observed: ''One of the distinct values of Wood's book is in the many places where he points out errors and misinterpretations in Ronald Gregor Smith's translation of *I and Thou.* [Unfortunately Walter Kaufmann's new translation had not yet appeared when Wood wrote his analysis.] For example, he clears up one of the most confusing passages in *I and Thou* . . . 'geistige Wesenheiten.' '' Maurice Friedman, ''The Ontology of the Between,'' a review of Robert E. Wood, *Martin Buber's Ontology* in *Review of Existential Psychiatry*, Vol. 11, No. 3, 1972, p. 184. Kaufmann, however, stayed with ''spiritual beings,'' much to the dismay and surprise of his readers. Other grammatical possibilities would include ''spiritual existences,'' ''spirit in phenomenal forms,'' in addition to Smith's early ''intelligible forms.'' The best proposal of all, however, is ''forms of the spirit,'' suggested by Robert Wood(p. 43), and endorsed by Friedman (*op. cit.*, p. 184). ''Forms of the spirit'' seems, more easily than others, and surely more easily than ''spiritual beings,'' to point the reader to the realm of art and idea that Buber had in mind.

4. Walter Kaufmann, ''Prologue to Martin Buber's *I and Thou*, p. 28.

5. Bryan J. Fair, ''Martin Buber and Some Theologians of 'Encounter,' '' *Scottish Journal of Theology*, Vol. 21, No. 1, March 1968, p. 29.

6. Will Herberg, ''Introduction,'' *The Writings of Martin Buber*, ed. Will Herberg (New York: New American Library, 1974), p. 14.

7. Paul Arthur Schilpp and Maurice Friedman, eds., ''Editors' Preface,'' *The Philosophy of Martin Buber — The Library of Living Philosophers* (LaSalle, Illinios: Open Court Publishing Company, 1967), p. xvii.

8. Charles Hartshorne, ''Martin Buber's Metaphysics,'' in *The Philosophy of Martin Buber — The Library of Living Philosphers*, ed. Paul Arthur Schilpp and Maurice Friedman, pp. 49-68; esp. pp. 55-56.

9. Nathan Rotenstreich, ''The Right and the Limitations of Buber's Dialogical Thought,'' in *Philosphy of Martin Buber — The Library of Living Philosophers*, p. 97.

10. Michael Wyschogrod, "Martin Buber," in *Encyclopedia of Philosophy,* ed. Paul Edwards (New York: Macmillan, 1967), Vol. 1, p. 410.

11. Eugene B. Borowitz, "The Legacy of Martin Buber," *Union Seminary Quarterly Review,* Vol. XXII, No. 1, November 1966, pp. 3-17.

12. Maurice S. Friedman, *Martin Buber: The Life of Dialogue* (New York: Harper Torchbooks, 1960). See esp. pp. 78-81, 169-171.

13. Maurice S. Friedman, "Introduction" to Martin Buber *Daniel: Dialogues on Realization* (New York: McGraw-Hill 1965), pp. 3-44.

14. Robert E. Wood, *Martin Buber's Ontology* (Evanston: Northwestern University Press, 1969), pp. 45-48, 78-79.

15. Wood, p. 45.

16. Martin Buber, "Man and His Image-Work," in *Knowledge of Man* (New York: Harper Torchbooks, 1965), pp. 149-165.

17. See Maurice Friedman, *Martin Buber and the Theater* (New York: Funk and Wagnalls, 1969).

18. Martin Buber, *The Origin and Meaning of Hasidism* (New York: Harper Torchbooks, 1966), p. 99.

19. Martin Buber, "Replies to My Critics," in *The Philosophy of Martin Buber—The Library of Living Philosophers,* p. 743.

20. Martin Buber, "Distance and Relation," in *Knowledge of Man* (New York: Harper Torchbooks, 1965), p. 68, n. 1.

21. *I and Thou,* trans. Kaufmann, p. 136.

22. Martin Buber, "Interrogation of Martin Buber," in *Philosophical Interrogations,* ed. Sydney Rome and Beatrice Rome (New York: Harper Torchbooks, 1970), p. 62.

23. This omission should not jeopardize the argument or conclusion of this chapter, since most of Buber's biblical discussions deal with fixed elements of the biblical sagas in their historicizing function (sea of reeds, burning bush); with an elaboration of constitutive metaphors (the beautiful reflection on "I bore you upon eagles' wings and brough you unto me"); or with mythical images (the talking ass of Balaam).

24. *I and Thou,* trans. Kaufmann, pp. 172-173.

25. Martin Buber "Dialogue," in *Between Man and Man* (New York: Macmillan, 1965), p. 1.

26. Martin Buber, *Daniel: Dialogues on Realization* (New York: McGraw-Hill, 1965), p. 139.

27. Buber, *Daniel,* p. 135.

28. *Ibid.,* p. 108.

29. *Ibid.,* p. 81.

30. Martin Buber, "Über Jakob Boehme," *Wiener Rundschau,* Vol. V,

No. 1, June 15, 1901, p. 253.

31. *Ibid.*

32. *Ibid.*

33. *Ibid.,* p. 252.

34. *Ibid.*

35. Jacob Boehme, *The Signature of All Things*[with other writings] (New York: E. P. Dutton and Co. 1912). See e.g., pp. 11-12: "... man in his speech, will, and behaviour, also with the form of the members he has, and must use to that signature, his inward form is noted in the form of his face; and thus also in a beast, an herb, and the trees; everything as it is inwardly so it is outwardly signed; and though it falls out, that often a thing is changed from evil into good, and from good into evil, yet it has its external character, that the good or evil . . . may be known."

36. Martin Buber, "On the Landscapes of Leopold Krakauer," in *A Believing Humanism: My Testament 1902-1965* (New York: Simon and Schuster, 1967), p. 108.

37. *Ibid.,* p. 106.

38. Buber, "Dialogue," pp. 22-23.

39. *I and Thou,* trans. Kaufmann, p. 145.

40. *Ibid.*

41. *Ibid.,* p. 57.

42. *Ibid.,* pp. 144-145.

43. Buber, "Interrogation of Martin Buber," p. 47.

44. *Ibid.,* p. 17

45. *Ibid.,* p. 21.

46. *I and Thou,* trans Kaufmann, p. 172.

47. Buber, "Interrogation of Martin Buber," p. 28.

48. *I and Thou,* trans, Kaufmann, p. 172.

49. Buber, "Dialogue," p. 10.

50. Buber, "Interrogation of Martin Buber," p. 23.

51. Buber, *Daniel,* pp. 127-128.

52. *Ibid.,* p. 131.

53 *Ibid.,* p. 138.

54. *Ibid.,* p. 134.

55. *Ibid.,* pp. 140-141.

56. *I and Thou,* trans. Kaufmann, pp. 146-147.

57. Buber, "Author's Preface," *Daniel,* p. 47.

58. Buber, *Daniel,* p. 54.

59. *I and Thou,* trans Kaufmann, pp. 56-59.

60. Martin Buber, "What Is Man?," in *Between Man and Man* (New

York: Macmillan, 1965), pp. 177-178.

61. Buber, "Man and His Image-Work," pp. 157-158.

62. Nan Hirleman, "It is All Right There," *Reflection* [Yale Divinity School], Vol. 72, No. 1, November 1974, pp. 13-14.

63. *Ibid.,* p. 14.

64. *I and Thou,* trans. Kaufmann, p. 69.

65. *Ibid.,* p. 148.

66. Buber, "Distance and Relation," p. 62.

67. *Ibid.,* p. 62.

68. *Ibid.*

69. *Ibid.,* p. 64.

70. Buber, "On the Landscapes of Leopold Krakauer," p. 107.

71. Buber, "Distance and Relation," pp. 60-61. "Animals call to one another, but only man speaks to other men as independent and particular others." Friedman, *Buber: Life of Dialogue,* p. 81.

72. Jean-Paul Sartre, *Nausea,* trans. Lloyd Alexander (London: New Directions, 1949).

73. *Ibid.,* pp. 19-20.

74. *Ibid.,* pp. 170-174.

75. *Ibid.,* p. 177.

76. Grete Schaeder, *The Hebrew Humanism of Martin Buber,* trans. Noah J. Jacobs (Detroit: Wayne State University Press, 1973), p. 110.

77. Chaim Potok, "Martin Buber and the Jews," *Commentary,* Vol. 41. See Friedman, "Introduction" to *Daniel,* pp. 3-44.

78. Martin Buber, "The Man of Today and the Jewish Bible," in *Israel and the World* (New York: Schocken Books, 1963), p. 92.

79. Schaeder, p. 151.

80. Hartshorne, "Martin Buber's Metaphysics," pp. 55-56.

81. Pedro C. Sevilla, *God as Person in the Writings of Martin Buber* (Manila: Ateneo de Manila University, 1970), p. 57.

82. Anton C. Pegis, "The Notion of Man in the Context of Renewal," in *Theology of Renewal,* ed. L. K. Shook (New York: Herder and Herder, 1968), I, 264. Cited in Sevilla, p. 50. See also: "The human unity of man and nature is the first and most far-reaching consequence of the Thomistic conception of the oneness of soul and body in man." Pegis, p. 262.

83. E. L. Mascall, *Existence and Analogy* (London: Darton, Longmans, and Todd, 1966), p. 183.

84. Buber, "What Is Man?," p. 129.

85. *Ibid.,* p. 128.

86. Joseph E. Mulligan, "Teilhard and Buber," *Religion in Life,* Vol. 39,

No. 3, Autumn 1969.

87. *Ibid.*, p. 364.

88. Ian G. Barbour, "The Significance of Teilhard," *The Christian Century*, August 30, 1967, p. 1099. See also: "Absolutely inert and totally brute matter *does not exist*. Every element of the Universe contains, at least to an infinitesimal degree, some germ of inwardness and spontaneity, that is to say of consciousness." Pierre Teilhard de Chardin, *Let Me Explain*, ed. Jean-Pierre Demoulin (New York: Harper and Row, 1966), p. 42.

89. Pierre Teilhard de Chardin, *Hymn of the Universe* (New York: Harper and Row, 1969), p. 69.

90. Pierre Teilhard de Chardin, "The Confluence of Religions," *Theology Today*, Vol. 27, No. 1, April 1970, p. 64.

91. S. Daniel Breslauer, *The Chrysalis of Religion: A Guide to the Jewishness of Buber's "I and Thou"* (Nashville: Abingdon, 1980).

92. *Ibid.*, pp. 19-20.

93. *Ibid.*, p. 20.

94. See Wanda Warren Berry, "Judaism without Covenant: Breslauer and Buber," *Jewish Social Studies*, Vol. 45, No. 1, Winter 1983.

95. Buber, "Interrogation of Martin Buber," p. 27.

96. Friedman, *Buber: Life of Dialogue*, p. 169.

97. Buber, "On the Landscapes of Leopold Krakauer," p. 120.

98. Buber, "Interrogation of Martin Buber," p. 37.

99. *Ibid.*, p. 27.

100. Malcolm Diamond, *Martin Buber—Jewish Existentialist* (New York: Harper Torchbooks, 1968), p. 32.

101. Buber, "Interrogation of Martin Buber," p. 44.

102. *I and Thou*, trans Kaufman, p. 141.

103. Buber, "Interrogation of Martin Buber," p. 40.

104. Martin Buber, *On Zion: The History of an Idea* (London: Horowitz Publishing Co., 1973), p. 15.

105. Diamond, p. 30.

106. *I and Thou*, trans, Smith, p. 15.

107. *I and Thou*, trans. Kaufmann, p. 67.

108. Buber, "Interrogation of Martin Buber," pp. 38-39.

109. Gaston Bachelard, "Preface" to *Je et Tu*[Martin Buber, *Ich und Du*, trans G. Bianquis] (Paris: Aubier, 1969), p. 11.

110. Samuel Rodin, "The Environing Crises and the Underlying Crisis," *Mentalities*, Vol. 1, No. 2, 1983, pp. 20-25.

111. *Ibid.*, p. 20.

112. Buber, "Interrogation of Martin Buber," p. 47.

113. *I and Thou,* trans. Smith, p. 8.

Chapter II

1. Buber, *I and Thou,* trans. Kaufmann, p. 77.
2. Paul Louis Dolinsky, *Martin Buber's Philosophy of Dialogue* (Ann Arbor: University Microfilms, 1981), p. 13. Ph.D. dissertation, State University of New York at Buffalo.
3. Buber, *I and Thou,* trans Smith, p. 27.
4. *Ibid.,* p. 131.
5. Buber, "Interrogation of Martin Buber," p. 114.
6. *Ibid.,* p. 28.
7. Pedro C. Sevilla, *God as Person in the Writings of Martin Buber,* p. 45.
8. *Ibid.,* p. 56.
9. Dolinsky, p. 59.
10. *Ibid.,* p. 60.
11. Friedman, "Introduction" to *Daniel,* p. 33. Friedman quotes here Buber, *Between Man and Man,* pp. 96 ff.
12. Buber, "Interrogation of Martin Buber," p. 26.
13. *Ibid.,* p. 28.
14. *Ibid.,* p. 27.
15. Sevilla, p. 45.
16. Buber, *Between Man and Man,* Section III, "Education," pp. 83-117.
17. Buber, *I and Thou,* trans. Smith, p. 132.
18. Maurice Friedman, "Martin Buber's Concept of Education: A New Approach to College Teaching," *The Christian Scholar,* Vol. 40, No. 2, June 1957, pp. 109-116. The reference is found on page 109.
19. Buber, "Interrogation of Martin Buber," p. 66.
20. *Ibid.,* p. 66.
21. Schaeder, p. 329.
22. John R. Scudder, Jr., "Freedom with Authority: A Buber Model for Teaching," *Educational Theory,* Vol. 18, Spring 1968, p. 133.
23. F.H. Hilliard, "A Re-Examination of Buber's Address on Education," *British Journal of Educational Studies,* Vol. 21, February 1973, pp. 40-49.
24. Edward David Kiner, "Some Problems in a Buber Model for Teaching," *Educational Theory,* Vol. 19, Fall 1969, p. 402.
25. Aubrey Hodes, *Martin Buber: An Intimate Portrait* (New York:

Viking Press, 1971), p. 117.

26. Eugene B. Borowitz, "Education is Not I-Thou," *Religious Education*, Vol. 66, September-October 1971, p. 331. He laments the fact that Buber never examined at length "the concept of role," i.e., of social expectation (p. 330).

27. Buber, "Interrogation of Martin Buber," p. 66.

28. Unfortunately, Buber did not give any sustained attention to curriculum: substance, process, development. See Haim Gordon, "Would Martin Buber Endorse the Buber Model?" *Educational Theory*, Vol. 23, No. 3, Summer 1973, p. 221.

29. Buber, *I and Thou*, trans. Smith, p. 133.

30. Buber, "Interrogation of Martin Buber," p. 60. Cf. Adolf Guggen-bühl-Craig, *Power in the Helping Professions* (New York: Spring Publications, 1971), p. 49: "The therapist exercises his healing function not as a computer but as a human being."

31. Cf.: "All over the world, it is being recognized today that what is being treated is not a symptom, but a patient." C. G. Jung, *The Undiscovered Self*, trans. R. F. C. Hull (Boston: Little, Brown, and Co., 1958), p. 12.

32. Martin Buber, "Healing through Meeting," in *A Believing Humanism* (New York: Simon and Schuster, 1967), pp. 138-143.

33. Buber, *I and Thou*, trans. Smith, p. 133.

34. Robert L. Katz, "Martin Buber and Psychotherapy," *Hebrew Union College Annual*, Vol. 46, 1975, p. 426.

35. Kenneth U. Gutsch and Howard S. Rosenblatt, "Counselor Education: A Touch of Martin Buber's Philosophy," *Counselor Education and Supervision*, September 1973, p. 11.

36. *Ibid.*, p.11.

37. Guggenbühl-Craig, *Power in the Helping Professions* (New York: Spring Publications, 1971).

38. *Ibid.*, p. 63.

39. Maurice Friedman, "The Existential Man: Buber," in *The Educated Man: Studies in the History of Educational Thought*, ed. Paul Nash, Andreas M. Kazamias, and Henry J. Perkinson (New York: John Wiley and Sons, 1965), p. 372.

40. Güggenbuhl-Craig, p. 64.

41. *Ibid.*, p. 14.

42. *Ibid.*, p. 62.

43. Buber, *I and Thou*, trans. Smith, p. 133.

44. Buber, "Healing through Meeting," p. 139. See also Friedman's use of the general expression "pastor and congregant," commonly appearing in

contemporary Judaism. Maurice Friedman, "Dialogue and the 'Essential We' — The Bases of Values in the Philosophy of Martin Buber," *American Journal of Psychoanalysis*, Vol 20, 1960, p. 30.

45. Buber, *I and Thou*, trans. Kaufmann, p. 179.

46. Zvi E. Kurzweil, "Buber on Education," *Judaism*, Vol. 11, 1962, p. 48.

47. Perry LeFevre, "Heidegger and Buber on Conscience and Guilt," *The Chicago Theological Seminary Register*, Vol. 52, No. 1, January 1962, p. 29

48. Friedman notes how in Macleish's play *JB* the priest-comforter deals with JB's situation only in categories of "original sin," rather than dealing with the particularity present, and suggests how this may be analogous to the various psychological conceptual models sometimes employed in the therapeutic situations. Friedman, "The Existential Man," p. 374.

In his analysis of Martin Buber as a "prophet of religious secularism," Donald Moore endeavors to locate and trace two sources for Buber's criticism of institutional religion. One source is the Jewish religious heritage itself, in biblical and Hasidic tradtions especially. The second is Buber's own philosophy of personalism, which, of course, has its own dialectical relation to the Jewish envisagement of the way to be religious. In his treatment of the second source, Moore analyzes the way of mutuality but does not deal at all with normative limitations. Such a consideration might have been expected, since the objectivity of this conception of the priest-penitent relationship is similar to the objectivities in religion against which Buber protested in the spirit of religion. Donald J. Moore, *Martin Buber, Prophet of Religious Secularism* (Philadelphia: The Jewish Publication Society of America, 1974).

49. Buber, *I and Thou*, trans. Smith, pp. 133-134. Cf.: ". . . a situation defined by the attempt of one partner to act on the other so as to accomplish some goal. . . ." Buber, *I and Thou*, trans. Kaufmann, p. 179.

50. Buber, *I and Thou*, trans. Smith, p. 11.

51. Buber, "Healing through Meeting," p. 138.

52. Friedman, "The Essential We," p. 31.

53. Harvey Cox, *The Secular City* (New York: Macmillan Co., 1965), p. 48.

54. *Ibid.*, pp. 48-49, 263.

55. Buber, *Between Man and Man*, p. 36.

56. Walter Kaufman, "I and You — A Prologue," in Buber, *I and Thou*, trans. Kaufmann, p. 17.

57. *Ibid.*, p. 16.

58. Immanuel Kant, *The Moral Law*, trans. H. J. Paton (London: Hutchinson and Co., 1948), p. 96.

59. Guggenbühl-Craig, p. 223.

60. *Ibid.*, p. 14.

61. Borowitz, p. 327. Katz also speaks of the "healing relationship of master and disciple," p. 414.

62. Guggenbühl-Craig, p. 79.

63. Margaret J. Rioch, "The Meaning of Martin Buber's 'Elements of the Interhuman' for the Practice of Psychotherapy," *Psychiatry*, Vol. 23, 1960, p. 133.

64. Maurice Friedman, "Healing Though Meeting: A Dialogical Approach to Psychotherapy and Family Therapy," in *Psychiatry and the Humanities*, ed. Joseph H. Smith (New Haven and London: Yale University Press, 1976), I, p.205.

65. Carl Frankenstein, "Buber's Theory of Dialogue: A Critical Re-examination," *Cross Currents*, Vol. 18, No. 2, Spring 1968, p. 230.

66. Friedman, "Healing Though Meeting," p. 212.

67. Guggenbühl-Craig, p. 91.

68. This was what Rogers insisted upon as a necessity in his famous discussion with Buber, and it does not seem to the present writer to be at all inconsistent with the asymmetrical nature of the helping relationships. See Friedman, "Healing Through Meeting," p. 209.

69. Guggenbühl-Craig, p. 130.

70. Kurzweil, p. 49.

71. Maurice Friedman, "Sex in Sartre and Buber," *Review of Existential Psychology and Psychiatry*, Vol. 10, No. 2, May 1963, pp. 113-124.

72. Haim Gordon, "A Method for Clarifying Buber's I-Thou Relationship," *Journal of Jewish Studies*, Vol. 27 (1976), pp. 71-83.

73. "Mis-meeting" was the term which Buber coined for what had occurred between him and his mother. Haim Gordon, "Did Buber Realize His Educational Thought?," *Teachers College Record*, Vol. 81, No. 3, 1980, p. 391.

74. Benjamin B. Wolman, "Buber, for Me," *Confrontation*, Vol. 2, Spring 1969, p. 52.

75. Hodes, p. 20.

76. *Ibid.*, p. 118.

77. *Ibid*, p. 121.

78. *Ibid.*, p. 127.

79. Dolinsky, pp. 62, 72.

80. Gordon, "Did Buber Realize . . .," p. 385.

81. *Ibid.*, p. 386.

82. Stephen Zweig, *The World of Yesterday* (London: Cassel and Co., 1943), as cited in Gordon, "Did Buber Realize . . .," p. 386.

83. See Buber, *I and Thou,* trans Smith, p. 34.

84. Friedman, "Foreword" to Moore, *Martin Buber, Prophet of Religious Secularism*, p. xiv.

85. Buber, *I and Thou,* trans. Smith, pp. 133-134.

86. Buber, *I and Thou,* trans. Kaufmann, p. 179.

87. The contrast I have suggested between "relationship" and "relation" as a way of clarifying the possibility of mutuality in task-defined meetings may have only provisional usefulness, since the same distinction has sometimes been made to represent the contrast between I-Thou ("relation") and I-It ("relationship"). My suggestion is simply one way to conceptualize the relational possibilities within a relation or situation of a task-defined meeting.

88. Buber, *I and Thou,* trans. Smith, p. 112.

89. *Ibid.,* p. 144.

90. Maurice Friedman's masterful and comprehensive three volume work provides a careful delineation of the way in which Buber's thought emerged in relation to all that he met and all that met him. Friedman describes his work as "a witness to one who has shown us 'the way of man' in a time when both our personal uniqueness and our humanity are in jeopardy. Martin Buber's significance for us is not that he was a saint or a *zaddik* or even one to whom the life of dialogue came easily, but rather that he was a person who embodied the contradictions and ambiguities of modern existence and yet was able again and again to reach personal wholeness and integrity in faithful response to the persons and situations of his time." Maurice Friedman, *Martin Buber's Life and Work: The Early Years*, p. xix. See also *Martin Buber's Life and Work: The Middle Years* (1983); *The Later Years* (1984).

Chapter III

1. Rosemary Radford Ruether, *To Change the World* (New York: Crossroad Publishing Co., 1981), especially chapter 3, "Christology and Jewish-Christian Relations," pp. 31-43; also, *Faith and Fractricide* (New York: Seabury Press, 1974).

2. Paul Van Buren, *Discerning the Way* (New York: Crossroad Publishing Company, 1980).

3. An epithet Buber used in the preface to his study of the founder of Hasidism. Martin Buber, *The Legend of Baal Shem Tov* (New York: Harper and Brothers; and London: East and West Library. 1955), p. xi.

4. Martin Buber, "Spinoza, Sabbatai Zvi, and the Baal-Shem," in Martin Buber, *The Origin and Meaning of Hasidism*, ed. and trans. Maurice Friedman (New York: Harper Torchbooks, 1966), p. 93.

5. Schaeder, p. 393.

6. Friedman, *Martin Buber: Life of Dialogue*, p. 269.

7. Malcolm Diamond, "Martin Buber and Contemporary Theology," *Union Seminary Quarterly Review*, Vol. 12, No. 2, January 1957, p. 23.

8. John C. Bennett, "Editorial Notes," *Christianity and Crisis*, Vol. 15, No. 24, January 23, 1956, p. 186.

9. Martin Buber, "Letter to Gandhi," in Martin Buber, *Pointing the Way*, ed. and trans. Maurice Friedman (New York: Harper Torchbooks, 1963), p. 146.

10. M.A. Beek and J. Sperna Weiland, *Martin Buber: Personalist and Prophet* (Westminster, Maryland: Newman Press, 1968), p. 86.

11. Martin Buber, *A Believing Humanism: My Testament 1902-1965* (New York: Simon and Schuster, 1967), p. 55.

12. *Ibid.*, p. 109. He is agreeing here with Leonhard Ragaz, who "knows that Moses, the prophets, and Jesus do not mean a religion, but a kingdom, a condition of the world in accord with God." *Ibid.*

13. Martin Buber, *Moses: The Revelation and the Covenant* (New York: Harper Torchbooks, 1958), p. 123.

14. Buber, *I and Thou*, trans. Smith, pp. 66-67.

15. Presumably referring here to Albert Schweitzer and possibly to Jacob Boehme (Cf. Martin Buber, "Über Jacob Boehme," *Weiner Rundschau*, Vol. V, No. 12, 1901, pp. 251-253.)

16. Potok, "Martin Buber and the Jews," p. 46.

17 Martin Buber, "Christ, Hasidism, and Gnosis," in Buber, *The Origin and Meaning of Hasidism*, p. 251.

18. Martin Buber, *Two Types of Faith: A Study of the Interpenetration of Judaism and Christianity* (New York: Harper Torchbooks, 1961), pp. 12-13.

19. Alexander S. Kohanski, "Martin Buber's Approach to Jesus," *Princeton Seminary Bulletin*, Vol. 67, No. 1, Winter 1975, pp. 103-115. Also, Alexander S. Kohanski, *Martin Buber's Philosophy of Interhuman Relation* (East Brusnwick, N. Y.: Associated University Presses, 1982). Although I reject his conclusions and take issue with his approach, I am indebted to Professor Kohanski's provocative essay for several suggestions which I have sought to develop from a very different standpoint.

20. Kohanski, "Martin Buber's Approach to Jesus," p. 114.

21. Paul Tillich, a contemporary of Buber in many ways, made use of a

similar distinction: "Polytheism is a qualitative and not a quantitative concept. It is not the belief in a plurality of gods but rather the lack of a uniting and transcending ultimate which determines its character." Paul Tillich, *Systematic Theology* (Chicago: The University of Chicago Press, 1951), I, 222. See David Miller's more recent utilization of this distinction in his *The New Polytheism* (New York: Macmillan, 1974), pp. 62-63.

22. Buber, "Spinoza, Sabbatai Zvi, and the Baal-Shem," p. 91.

23. *Ibid.,* p. 94.

24. *Ibid.*

25. Buber, *Moses,* p. 127.

26. *Ibid.*

27. Gerard S. Sloyan, "Buber and the Significance of Jesus," in *The Bridge,* ed. John M. Oestrreicher (New York: Pantheon, 1958), III, 213, n. 23.

28. Martin Buber, "Imitatio," in Martin Buber, *Israel and the World* (New York: Schocken Books, 1963), p. 68. Buber does not develop the distinction between these transformationist categories, including "deification," and juridical categories, such as "redemption," which he sees as definitive of and central to Christian faith. A different way of viewing the distinction between Judaism and Christianity might have followed were he to have done so, although both conceptual patterns are an affront to much of Jewish religiousness.

29. Buber, *Two Types of Faith,* p. 150, n. 1.

30. Sloyan, p. 212.

31. Martin Buber, "Jewish Mysticism," in Martin Buber, *Tales of Rabbi Nachman* (New York: Avon Books, 1956), p. 17.

32. Buber, *I and Thou,* trans. Smith, pp. 66-69, 86-95. See Werner Manheim, *Martin Buber* (New York: Twayne Publishers, Inc., 1974), p. 47.

33. Schaeder, p. 99.

34. *Ibid.,* p. 393.

35. *Ibid.,* p. 91.

36. *Ibid.,* p. 101.

37. *Ibid.,* p. 13.

38. Buber, *Two Types of Faith,* p. 128.

39. *Ibid.,* p. 172.

40. Schaeder, p. 398.

41. Buber, *Two Types of Faith,* p. 124.

42. Maurice Friedman, "Martin Buber's Credo," in Martin Buber, *A Believing Humanism,* p. 21.

43. *Ibid.,* p. 22.

44. Buber, "Spinoza, Sabbatai Zvi, and the Baal-Shem," p. 92.

45. Buber, *Two Types of Faith,* p. 115.

46. *Ibid.,* p. 170. Cf. "The resurrection of an individual person does not belong to the realm of ideas of the Jewish world" (Buber, *Two Types of Faith,* p. 128).

47. *Ibid.,* p. 15.

48. Martin Buber, "The Foundation Stone," in Martin Buber, *The Origin and Meaning of Hasidism,* p. 88.

49. Martin Buber, "Redemption," in Martin Buber, *The Origin and Meaning of Hasidism,* p. 205.

50. Schaeder, p. 134.

51. Buber, *Two Types of Faith,* pp. 173-174.

52. *Ibid.,* p. 11.

53. *Ibid.*

54. Schaeder, p. 396.

55. Buber, "Spinoza, Sabbatai Zvi, and the Baal-Shem," p. 107.

56. *Ibid.,* p. 111.

57. Martin Buber, *Werke III: Schriften zum Chassidismus* (Heidelberg: Lambert Schneider, 1963), p. 1260. See also Buber, *Two Types of Faith,* p. 107. Buber develops the themes of servanthood and silence from Isaiah 49:2b-3a:

". . .in the shadow of his hand he hid me;

he made me a polished arrow,

    and in his quiver he hid me away.

And he said to me, 'You are my servant.'"

58. Potok, p. 49.

59. Martin Buber, *Werke I: Schriften zur Philosophie* (Munich: Kosel-Verlag, and Heidelberg: Lambert Schneider, 1962), p. 763.

60. Beek and Weiland, p. 97.

61. Buber, "Spinoza, Sabbatai Zvi, and the Baal-Shem," p. 109.

62. Martin Buber, "Spirit and Body of the Hasidic Movement," in Martin Buber, *The Origin and Meaning of Hasidism,* p. 130.

63. Martin Buber, *The Two Foci of the Jewish Soul* (New York: Schocken Books, 1963), p. 39.

64. Buber, "Spirit and Body of the Hasidic Movement," p. 129.

65. Buber, "Spinoza, Sabbatai Zvi, and the Baal-Shem," pp. 109-110. Buber apparently felt this passage to have a special significance, for he quotes it again in his essay, "Christ, Hasidism, and Gnosis," p. 250.

66. Kohanski, "Martin Buber's Approach to Jesus," p. 114.

67. See, for example, W. D. Davies, *Paul and Rabbinic Judaism* (London: S.P.C.K., 1948).

68. Sloyan, p. 231. See also e.g., the following: "The Jewish world into which Jesus was born was one of great diversity and variety. . . . theologically the Jews were pursuing a quest along many different paths for the meaning and application of their faith. In fact, there is a sense in which it is true to say that at the time when Jesus was born, there was no such thing as 'Judaism'; instead there were a variety of ways in which Jews sought to define what Judaism ought to become and be, in their own time and generation" (John Bowker, *Problems of Suffering in Religions of the World* [Cambridge: Cambridge University Press, 1970], p. 42). Also ". . . any attempt to understand the teaching (and life) of Jesus and the emergence of early Christianity must take into account the extent to which they were an interpretation, one among many, of what Judaism should be. They belong, first and foremost, to the variety and diversity of the Jewish world" (p. 44). See also John Bowker, *Targums and Rabbinic Literature: An Introduction to Jewish Interpretations of Scripture* (Cambridge: Cambridge University Press, 1969).

69. Buber, *Werke I*, p. 754; cf. Buber, *Two Types of Faith*, p. 137.

70. Beek and Weiland, p. 92.

71. For example, Joachim Jeremias' discussion of Jesus' use of *abba* and *amen*. Joachim Jeremias, *The Central Message of the New Testament* (New York: Charles Scribner's Sons, 1965), pp. 9-30; Joachim Jeremias, "The Lord's Prayer in Modern Research," *Expository Times,* 71, 1960, pp. 141-146; expanded versions of these approaches are found in Joachim Jeremias, *The Prayers of Jesus* (London: SMC Press, 1967), Studies in Biblical Theology, Second Series, No. 6. "Thus the life and teaching of Jesus belong to Judaism, yet they represent an individual and independent interpretation of it." (Bowker, *Problems of Suffering,* p. 45).

72. As Kohanski noted but did not develop. Kohanski "Martin Buber's Approach to Jesus," p. 105.

73. Malcolm Diamond, *Martin Buber, Jewish Existentialist* (New York: Oxford University Press, 1960), p. 174.

74. ". . . he [Buber] had to judge historical movements polemically. . . . Official Judaism of the past was used by him as a foil for the institutional Judaism of the present . . . and the spiritualized tendencies of the past, which seemed to challenge the existing order and even to rebel against it, were presented as true" (Nahum Glatzer, "Editor's Postscript," in Martin Buber, *On Judaism,* ed. Nahum Glatzer (New York: Schocken Books, 1967), pp. 240-241).

75. Jacob Neusner, *A Life of Rabban Yohanan Ben Zakkai, ca. 1-90 C.E.* (Leiden: E. J. Brill, 1962). An abridgement and condensation of this important work has recently appeared: Jacob Neusner, *First Century Judaism in Crisis* (Nashvile: Abingdon Press, 1975).

76. James Muilenberg, "Buber as an Interpreter of the Bible," in *The Philosophy of Martin Buber,* ed. Paul Arthur Schilpp and Maurice Friedman p. 382.

77. Martin Buber, "Höre, Israel," quoted in Beek and Weiland, p. 87.

78. As witnessed by the work of such futurist theologians as Moltmann, Pannenberg, Teilhard de Chardin, and Benz; e.g., Jurgen Moltmann, *Theology of Hope* (New York: Harper and Row. 1975) (paperback edition) and Ernst Benz, *Evolution and Christian Hope* (Garden City, New York: Doubleday Anchore Books, 1968).

79. Two of the many areas in which such a looking together at "Jesus the common brother" might have some positive benefit are the academic and political. (1) Many Jewish and Christian students of the New Testament are fascinated by the discovery that the central figure of those apostolic writings is not the deracinated Jew that some forms of piety might have led them to think was the case. (2) The theological significance of the State of Israel for Christian self-understanding has possibilities for adding depth to the Jewish-Christian encounter. No Christian can live in Israel for any time without an increased awareness of both the Jewishness of Jesus and the courage of his struggle against Pharasaic Judaism. The respect and love for Jesus' people as well as sympathy and support for Israel's right to life need a grounding more substantial, however, than reawakened memories. The picture of Jesus as the "common brother" might be just the sort of light that would give the needed seriousness and objectivity to these commitments.

Chapter IV

1. Martin Buber, *Paths in Utopia* (Boston: Beacon Press, 1958), p. 8.

2. Buber, *Paths in Utopia,* p. 15.

3. Buber, *Paths in Utopia,* p. 139.

4. Buber's judgment that there are "gradations" of mutuality is paralleled by his observation that there are gradations of objectification as well. ". . . there are, to be sure, different stages of the I-It state, according to how far it is alienated from the I-Thou relation and gives up the pointing back to it." Martin Buber, "Replies to My Critics," in Schilpp and Friedman, eds., *The Philosophy of Martin Buber,* p. 724.

5. Buber, "Replies to My Critics," p. 743.

INDEX OF PROPER NAMES

Aquinas, Thomas   30

Bachelard, Gaston   37, 108
Barbour, Ian   108
Beek, M.A.   114, 117,
    118
Bennett, John   72, 114
Benz, Ernst   118
Berry, Wanda Warren xiii, 108
Boehme, Jacob   6-9, 16, 27,
    106, 114
Borowitz, Eugene   3, 46, 47,
    59, 105, 109, 112
Bowker, John   117
Breslauer, S. Daniel   27, 32, 33,
    108
Buddha   77

Cohn, Margot   xiii
Cox, Harvey   54-56, 111

Davies, W.D.   117
Diamond, Malcolm   27, 34, 72,
    85, 108, 114, 117
Dilthey, Wilhelm   27
Dolinsky, Paul   109, 112

Eckhart, Meister   27
Empedocles   15

Fair, Bryan   2, 104
Feuerbach, Ludwig   8
Frank, Jacob   81
Frankenstein, Carl   60, 112
Freud, Sigmund   ix, 48
Friedman, Maurice   3, 27, 36,
    44, 51, 59, 61, 65, 78, 103-115
Fromm, Erich   48

Gandhi, Mohandas K. 72
Glatzer, Nahum   117
Goethe, Johann Wolfgang 77

Gordon, Haim 61-63, 109, 112

Guggenbühl-Craig, Adolf 49, 59, 109, 110, 112

Gutsch, Kenneth 48, 49, 110

Hartshorne, Charles 2, 28, 104, 107

Herberg, Will 2, 104

Hilliard, F.H. 46, 109

Hirleman, Nan 20, 107

Hocking, W.E. 38

Hodes, Aubrey 62, 109, 112

Horney, Karen 48

Hutchins, Robert 47

Jeremias, Joachim 117

Jung, Carl G. 48, 110

Kant, Immanuel 37, 56-58, 112

Katz, Robert 110, 112

Kaufmann, Walter xii, 2, 27, 50, 51, 54, 56, 57, 65, 103, 104, 111

Kazamias, Andreas M. 110

Kiner, Edward 46, 109

Kohanski, Alexander 74, 86, 114-117

Krakauer, Leopold 8, 9, 14

Kurtzweil, Zvi 51, 111, 112

Lao-Tzu 77

LeFevre, Perry 111

Levinas, Emmanuel 33, 44

Luther, Martin 72

MacLeish, Archibald 111

Manheim, Werner 115

Marcel, Gabriel 1

Marx, Karl ix

Mascall, Eric 30, 107

Mead, George 1

Miller, David 115

Moltmann, Jurgen 114, 118

Moore, Donald J. 64, 111

Moses 73, 75

Muilenberg, James 87, 118

Mulligan, Joseph 107

Nash, Paul 110

Neusner, Jacob 118

Nicholas of Cusa 27

Niebuhr, Reinhold 92

Oesterreicher, John M. 115

Oldham, J.H. xi, 103

Pannenberg, Wolfhart 118

Pegis, Anton 29, 107

Perkinson, Henry J. 110

Pfuetze, Paul 93

Philo 76

Potok, Chaim 27, 73, 82, 107, 114

Rabbi Nachman of Bratzlav 76

Ragaz, Leonhard 114

Riesman, David 48

Rioch, Margaret 59, 112

Rodin, Samuel 38, 108, 110

Rome, Beatrice 105

Rome, Sydney 105

Rosenblatt, Howard S. 48, 49, 110
Rotenstreich, Nathan 2, 104
Ruether, Rosemary Radford 71, 113

Sartre, Jean Paul   23, 26, 107
Schaeder, Grete   26-28, 107,
                        109, 114-116
Schilpp, Paul Arthur   104, 118
Scudder, John   46, 109
Schweitzer, Albert   73
Sevilla, Pedro   29, 107, 109
Simon, Ernst   69
Sloyan, Gerald   84, 115, 117
Smith, Joseph H.   112
Smith, Ronald Gregor   xii, xiii, 65,
                        104
Socrates   76
St. Francis of Assisi   8

Teilhard de Chardin   31, 32, 108,
                        118
Thieme, Karl   72
Tillich, Paul   114, 115
Titus   86

Van Buren, Paul   71, 113

Weiland, J. Sperna   114, 117,
                        118
Wolman, Benjamin   62, 112
Wood, Robert   3, 104, 105
Wyschogrod, Michael   2, 104

Zvi, Sabbatai   81
Zweig, Stephan   63, 113